Comprehension Lessons for

RTI

Grades 3–5

Assessments, Intervention Lessons, and Management
Tips to Help You Reach and Teach Tier 2 Students

Elizabeth Stein

SCHOLASTIC

New York • Toronto • London • Auckland • Sydney
Mexico City • New Delhi • Hong Kong • Buenos Aires

Dedication

As far back as I can remember—to those musical moments that started it all . . .

Acknowledgements

So many thanks to the great minds in education, past and present, who serve as an inspiration and have guided me to deepen my understanding of great instruction within an RTI framework. They include Lev Vygotsky, John Dewey, Donald Schon, Douglas Fuchs, Richard Allington, and Robert Marzano. Additional thanks to my colleagues at the Teacher Leaders Network, whose brilliance has always pushed my thinking along truly inspirational pathways.

Thanks to John Norton, the co-founder of Teacher Leaders Network and the founder and co-editor of *Middleweb*, who has the most unique touch of blending his comprehensive knowledge of education with his one and only magical editor's wand. In addition, John's creativity, humor, and collegial friendship have encouraged, supported, and inspired me to share and strengthen my voice over the years. I consider his influence to have had a personal, professional, and ongoing impact.

I thank my colleagues at Mills Pond Elementary School, a school filled with some of the best teacher minds around: to principal Arlene Wild, who shared her vision for what best practice looks like in classrooms and then made it happen; to Jeanne Hall and Mary Connors, who opened up their classrooms and their minds to new ways of teaching and learning together; to Stephanie Weinar, for being there whenever I needed a photo taken of the class; to Joyce Tyree, for our collaborative and collegial friendship as we worked to guide Mills Pond students to read with success.

This book benefited from two editors: Thanks to Joanna Davis-Swing for sharing her vision for writing this book and for guiding me through the initial stages. I also thank Sarah Glasscock, whose focus guided us through the production stage.

To Michael and my girls, who always support my zombie modes of researching, reading, and writing, who understand the time it takes for me to satisfy the passionate educator in me, and who know how to help me balance my many interests with my insatiable need to relax and enjoy our time together.

~ES

Cover design: Jorge Namerow
Interior Design: Sarah Morrow
Development Editor: Joanna Davis-Swing
Editor: Sarah Glasscock
Copyeditor: David Klein

ISBN: 978-0-545-29681-6

Contents

The Teacher as an Essential Component of Response to Intervention

When teachers speculate, reason, and contemplate using open-mindedness, whole-heartedness, and responsibility, they will act with foresight and planning rather than base their actions on tradition, authority, or impulse.

~John Dewey

The teacher is one of the most important components of Response to Intervention. Yes, that's right; we are a key determinant of students' success within the instructional process of RTI. Just think about it: We make the final decisions about how to organize and create the learning environment for our students. This awareness has a dual effect. It's very rewarding to be able to apply our knowledge and beliefs and do what we know is right for students. Yet, at the same time, this responsibility can be daunting, to say the least. It is only when we empower ourselves with the necessary knowledge and tools that we can empower our students. It is up to each of us; our beliefs, our attitudes, and our willingness to be flexible along the teaching and learning process are what will make RTI effective. We are the first responders and driving force as we welcome RTI into our classrooms. We have the most important role in providing students with opportunities to respond to instruction and intervention.

The RTI framework enables us to see the natural link between our instruction and student achievement. It allows us to organize our teaching and guides us to practice intentional instruction as we select appropriate instructional strategies to meet the needs of our students.

This book will provide you with a deeper understanding of RTI and Tier 2 instruction. You will be able to visualize what it could look like in your classroom and, most important, how to *apply* its systematic framework within your existing classroom structure. Undoubtedly, RTI will force some changes in your teaching experiences, so keep an open mind. These can be welcome changes, and they serve two important purposes.

- You will strengthen your knowledge of pedagogical beliefs and strategies, becoming an even stronger and more effective teacher than you are right now.

- Your students will have rich opportunities to achieve their personal best, which is what we strive for every day.

Educators around the nation are adopting RTI. As I read about how this initiative is being implemented throughout many districts, I cheer with satisfaction in some cases and wince with frustration in others. As a middle school special education teacher (who recently transferred from the elementary level), I have experienced RTI's slow but steady progress as it has made its way into the world of elementary schools. Now I am on the sidelines, waiting for it to become established within secondary schools as well. Some teachers are buying into the ideas of RTI, while others push back against this seemingly new initiative, thinking that it's just one more thing to do, that it is just a new buzzword they must begin integrating into their already busy lives. These fears can be laid to rest.

The ideas behind RTI have been around for many decades (dating back to Dewey and earlier educators), with roots firmly set in the history of special education. RTI was developed in the late 1970s by numerous researchers who felt that teaching and learning could only improve when teachers became diagnosticians committed to prescribing learning opportunities that met the needs of individual learners. This method, then called Diagnostic-Prescriptive Teaching, sought to prevent students from failing by providing individualized instruction.

The researchers in the 1970s believed that Diagnostic-Prescriptive Teaching was a valid way of identifying students with learning disabilities because it avoided the problems associated with the Discrepancy Model, which required educators to compare students' IQ scores with their academic performance. If students demonstrated a significant discrepancy between their performance and capabilities, then they would be identified as having a learning disability. The problem with the Discrepancy Model was that it took time to gather enough data to prove that a student was struggling. On the other hand, Diagnostic-Prescriptive Teaching, now known as RTI, prescribed early and intensive interventions in the regular educational setting, based on a student's learning characteristics, before referring him or her to special education. Although it is a tried-and-true framework, RTI *feels* new because it has been given a new name, and now general education teachers are being asked to apply it.

My best advice is to just go with the flow. RTI is here. It is a commonsense approach to teaching and learning. As Dr. William Bender (2009) states, "RTI is really the way every teacher has always wanted to teach."

This book will review RTI in its most basic form. My goal is to show you that RTI, in all its glory, is based on practices that you already have in place. The RTI strategies offered here can guide you to fine-tune and perfect your current practice. And the new aspects (such as progress monitoring and the use of research-based strategies) that undeniably go along with RTI will serve as a means to plan and implement effective instructional methods, while strengthening your teaching abilities and increasing student achievement.

Most of this book focuses on Tier 2 reading interventions that facilitate small-group instruction within the general education classroom. Tier 2 instruction can lead to powerful moments in the learning process for students who need additional support. In addition, you can collect meaningful performance data to ascertain individual needs and monitor a student's progress. Tier 2 instruction can make all the difference as you guide your students to achieve.

What Are Research-Based Strategies?

One of the greatest questions about RTI seems to be, "How do I know if an instructional strategy is research based?" The answer is very simple. If the strategy in question has peer-reviewed evidence of its effectiveness, then it is research-based. Robert Marzano's Six-Step Academic Vocabulary process (2004) is one strong example. If you are looking for vocabulary strategies, it is easy to find information on the strategies that Marzano's work has to offer. In addition, if you can find a given strategy discussed in a peer-reviewed journal with evidence of effective research, you know it is research based.

In order to integrate research-based strategies into your classroom, however, you must be sure to follow the classroom-tested procedures precisely as researchers lay them out. This is called teaching with fidelity, and it is a key factor of highly qualified teaching. Within the classroom environment of RTI instruction, fidelity is a natural process that occurs when you do the following:

- Adhere to the curriculum and assessment procedures as outlined by your chosen strategy
- Implement instruction systematically and explicitly to support students as needed
- Use specified instructional materials
- Link intervention strategies with targeted skills and intended outcomes
- Define responsibilities of students, teachers, and other instructional personnel

- Monitor students' progress through a systematic plan
- Inform all teachers working with a given student, and his or her parents, about the student's progress
- Collect data based on a student's performance
- Make decisions based on a student's performance data
- Participate in ongoing professional development

It's Not About the Program—It's About the Instruction!

Educators cannot simply buy a program, implement it, and say, "OK, we're doing RTI." It's not about the program—it's about the teaching behind the program. This book is directed at teachers who know their students so well that they put in the time to adopt research-based strategies and adapt them to the needs of their students. Packaged programs can be very helpful, particularly when it comes to organizing the assessment phase of instruction, but we must remember to be flexible. Packaged programs have a general population in mind, not our specific students. The teacher, not the program, is the most valuable component of a successful RTI experience. A program can outline the skills that need to be taught, but skills alone are not enough. If we allow these programs to drive our instruction, then we make the instructional process susceptible to becoming a contrived learning experience. We must remember that our instructional decisions are key to making learning meaningful for our students. We need to keep our focus on teaching the content, skills, and strategies that students need to be independent learners.

What's Inside This Book

Comprehension Lessons for RTI: Grades 3–5 was created for you, the busy middle-grade teacher who needs to understand the basics of RTI and how it could work in your classroom. Chapter 1 gives an overview of RTI, including a brief history of the process. It is important to note that while this book defines RTI along the typical three-tier model, some schools choose to vary the tiers framework. Regardless of the format, RTI enables schools to create a framework for improving student achievement.

As you begin to consider how RTI might fit into your own classroom, you can also begin to think about the value of reflective teaching processes. Chapter 2 outlines instructional structures designed to improve comprehension. Chapter 3 explores the importance of assessment and progress monitoring in the RTI framework, particularly in Tier 2 instruction. Chapter 4 focuses on vocabulary instruction and offers research-based strategies to apply in your classroom, while Chapters 5 and 6 focus on fluency and comprehension, respectively. Each lesson in Chapters 4–6 is stepped out and includes suggestions for formative assessments.

All the strategies shared in this book focus on reading because reading is a skill that students need in all content areas. It is a life skill. Too many upper-grade students are still literal-level thinkers. In addition, many struggling readers are also struggling writers. Yet, to become a proficient writer, one must first be able to read deeply and with purpose and motivation. And so, with an eye toward guiding students to becoming proficient readers and writers, I have filled this book with strategies that can help transform indifferent readers into independent, skilled, and passionate readers. Of course, writing is a part of a balanced literacy approach, but keeping the focus on reading rather than emphasizing writing can help relax an already struggling student. I hope that the writing strategies embedded within the strategic instruction in this book heighten your awareness and lighten your worries about implementing RTI into your daily teaching repertoire. You may come to see that what you are already doing in your classroom blends naturally within the framework of RTI. You will definitely expand your repertoire of strategies that can work both with whole-class instruction and within small-group/Tier 2 instructional time. So let's begin exploring the basics of RTI.

Chapter 1

Embracing Response to Intervention

The ultimate goal of education is student achievement. It is the efficacy of achieving student success that delineates good teachers, great teachers, and highly effective teachers. RTI's commonsense approach to teaching results in highly effective teachers who guide the individuals in their classrooms toward their personal best.

As you learn more about RTI, you will likely recognize ideas that you can connect to what you are already doing in the classroom. Once you understand the overall focus of RTI, you will notice many aspects of the process that you already incorporate in your daily practice. And ideally, the framework will broaden and strengthen your knowledge, awareness, and ability to provide high-quality instruction.

RTI: A Practical View

Response to Intervention is all about effective instruction that provides students with opportunities to meet academic and personal goals. It's about high-quality teaching and student achievement. RTI provides a framework for evaluating how students are responding to your instructional decisions and practices. Typically, teachers who follow a philosophy consistent with an RTI mind-set do the following:

- Implement lessons flexibly
- Engage students in the process of learning
- Observe students' learning behaviors within the moments of instructional time

- Use observations of student participation and work samples to plan for the next lesson

The foregoing characterize what effective teachers have been doing for decades. Another aspect of highly effective teaching is the ability to reflect on one's own teaching practice, so take a moment to apply your personal teaching experiences to what you know about RTI so far.

:: Reflect on how your teaching philosophy and practices connect to the practical definition of RTI.

:: Jot down specific teaching practices you are currently using that align with the RTI philosophy.

I hope that as you learn more about RTI, you will hear yourself say, "That sounds like something I can easily do to complement my classroom practices." Here are some ways that RTI will affect what you are already doing.

- You will learn to make sure your instructional practices are based on research that has proven effective in other classrooms.

- You will apply progress-monitoring techniques to ensure that students are responding to classroom instruction.

- You will collect data on student performance to inform your instructional decisions.

These are changes that, when embraced, will empower you and your students.

RTI: A Theoretical View

RTI has built-in assessment procedures to guide you in monitoring student learning. Assessment is ongoing and productive, allowing you to plan upcoming lessons based on student performance. Here are the key tenets of RTI.

- *High-quality, scientifically based classroom instruction.* All students receive high-quality, research-based instruction in the general education classroom.

- *Ongoing student assessment.* Screening and monitoring the progress of all students provides information about their learning rates and levels of achievement, both individually and compared with their peers. Teachers use this data to determine which students need closer monitoring or intervention, and they continually monitor student progress throughout the RTI process to assess student achievement and gauge the effectiveness of the curriculum. They base decisions regarding students' instructional needs on data gathered over time.

- *Consistent collaboration and a teamwork approach.* In order for students to achieve, educators and administrators must take a team approach to the educational process. We must think of our learners as "our students" rather than "my students." We must collaborate and share our expertise as we all strive to guide students to reach personal and academic achievements.

- *Parent involvement.* Schools implementing RTI provide parents with information about their children's progress, the instruction and interventions used, the staff who are delivering the instruction, and their children's academic or behavioral goals.

RTI is generally categorized as a three-tier model of support that applies research-based academic or behavioral instruction and interventions. The three tiers flow within a natural cycle of instruction that always includes the whole-class core instruction of Tier 1.

THE THREE TIERS OF RTI

In their simplest form, the RTI tiers look like this:

Tier 1: The first tier refers generally to whole-class instruction, yet, it can also include small-group instruction that meets once or twice a week. The key is that students learn through high-quality, research-based instructional practices with little or no additional accommodations.

Tier 2: The intensity of instruction increases through small-group instruction that meets at least three times per week. Instruction at Tier 2 supplements instruction for students who struggle during whole-class instruction. It is worth restating that Tier 1 is always a part of the RTI process for students who participate in Tiers 2 and 3.

Tier 3: If students continue to struggle during Tier 1 and Tier 2, the intensity of instruction increases through more frequent small-group instruction and in some cases one-on-one instructional time.

Tier 3
Individualized Instruction

Tier 2
Small-group Instruction

Tier 1
Whole-class Instruction

TIER 1: HIGH-QUALITY CLASSROOM INSTRUCTION, SCREENING, AND GROUP INTERVENTIONS

Within Tier 1, all students receive high-quality, scientifically based instruction from qualified personnel to ensure that their difficulties are not due to inadequate instruction. All students are screened within the first few weeks of a new school year (universal screening) to establish an academic and behavioral baseline and to identify struggling learners who need additional support. Students identified as being at risk through universal screenings and/or the results of state- or district-wide tests can receive additional small-group instruction during the school day, once or twice each week, in the regular classroom. This small-group time provides additional practice for them to apply the skills and strategies taught during the whole-class lesson. The length of time for this step can vary, but it generally should not exceed eight weeks. During this additional instructional intervention, teachers closely monitor student progress using a validated screening system such as curriculum-based measurements. At the end of this period, students who show progress indicating they no longer need additional support return to the regular classroom program. Students who do not show adequate progress generally move to Tier 2.

TIER 2: INCREASED INTENSITY AND DURATION OF TARGETED INSTRUCTION AND INTERVENTIONS

Students who continue to struggle within the whole-class setting of Tier 1 receive more intensive instruction that targets their needs based on performance level and rate of progress. This additional instruction takes place in small-group settings. In grades 3–5, academic interventions typically occur in the areas of reading and math. Teachers monitor student progress and gather data to show evidence of their learning. Generally, they monitor Tier 2 every 6–12 weeks. If a student does not demonstrate progress after a six-week intervention schedule, a teacher might decide that he or she just needs more time to demonstrate progress, perhaps another six weeks of intensive instruction. Again, the teacher must collect data to demonstrate both how the student is progressing and the integrity of the instructional methods being implemented. Students who continue to show too little progress at this level of intervention might require more intensive interventions as part of Tier 3.

   Tier 2 is a critical juncture in the learning process. If it is implemented effectively, many students may be able to return to the whole-class instruction model of Tier 1—without additional support. However, if a student continues to struggle even with an effective Tier 2 model in place, this could indicate a true learning disability—and a lack of ineffective instruction can be ruled out. Because Tier 2 instruction is so critical in the determination of a student's educational path, this book focuses on strategies and instructional support for applying Tier 2 instruction in your classroom.

TIER 3: MORE INTENSIVE INTERVENTIONS AND COMPREHENSIVE EVALUATION

Tier 3 intervention enters the scene when a student continues to demonstrate a lack of progress after the designated Tier 2 instruction and monitoring. Tier 3 deepens the instruction of Tier 1 and Tier 2 by increasing the intensity and frequency of instruction. For example, one-to-one instruction, rather than small-group instruction, might be implemented, and/or the amount of supplemental instruction might increase to four or five times per week rather than the three times per week of the Tier 2 model. Tier 3 instruction typically involves individualized, intensive interventions that target specific skill deficits. Students who do not achieve the desired level of progress in response to these targeted interventions are often referred for a comprehensive evaluation and considered for eligibility for special education services under the Individuals with Disabilities Education Improvement Act of 2004 (IDEA 2004). The eligibility decision is based on the data collected during each tier. At any point during the RTI process, IDEA 2004 allows parents to request a formal evaluation to determine their child's eligibility for special education. An RTI process may not delay or cause the denial of a formal evaluation for special education. For more information on RTI and IDEA 2004, please visit http://idea.ed.gov/explore/view/p/,root,dynamic,QaCorner,8.

Kicking Up the Instructional Intensity From Tier 1 to Tier 2

A few years ago, I attended a professional development course on differentiating instruction. The presenter opened with a simple analogy that connected meal planning with the mind-set that teachers need in order to plan effective core instruction. The analogy is as follows:

> *When planning a dinner for a large group of family and friends, you first think about what foods you will prepare. For the most part, you know that all of your guests enjoy your turkey with all the trimmings, so you begin to shop and plan for the meal. You then think about Aunt Bessie, who is diabetic, so you make sure there is something for her to eat. You also remember that Cousin Bert is a vegetarian, so you will need to make sure to provide for him. And then there are those picky nieces and nephews who have, so far, not acquired a sophisticated palate; you must make sure there will be kid-friendly foods as well. Once all is said and done, you've prepared one meal from the standpoint of meeting the needs of the individuals within the group you are entertaining. And everyone leaves the dining room table feeling satisfied.*

A Student Profile

Rachel is a third grader in a school that has just begun to pilot an RTI framework. It is September, and Rachel's teacher, Ms. Krasney, assesses her students' reading skills. The assessment reveals that Rachel demonstrates some gaps in her ability to comprehend text at grade level. Ms. Krasney meets with the other third-grade teachers to discuss all of their students who appear to be struggling. They brainstorm instructional methodologies that they might use to provide additional reading instruction for these students. As a result of this meeting, Ms. Krasney creates small-group instruction to meet the needs of Rachel and three other students. This small-group instruction takes place once each week for 30 minutes to support the skills taught during the daily whole-class literacy block instruction. This small-group time gives Ms. Krasney an up-close view of why these students are struggling within the whole-class setting. When she meets with these students, she sets up the rest of the class to work in groups or independently.

Ms. Krasney monitors the progress of her students every week, and the third-grade teachers continue to meet every two weeks. After six weeks of additional instruction, Ms. Krasney meets again with her colleagues to make sure the intervention selected for Rachel's group is working, before too many weeks go by.

After these six weeks of instruction, and three team meetings, the data on these students begins to tell a story. The team notices that two of the students are steadily progressing, but the progress demonstrated by Rachel and one other student is minimal. The team decides to discontinue additional instruction for the two students who are making progress and to continue the supplementary small-group instruction for Rachel and the other student. The team reviews the current instructional strategies and decides to introduce another strategy that may be more successful. Teachers continue to monitor the students' weekly progress through their notes, samples of students' work, and teacher-made assessments of student performance.

The team will meet in another four weeks to see if the change in instructional strategies has made an impact on Rachel and the other student. At that point, the teachers will decide whether this additional focused instruction within Tier 1 is working. If the students show some progress, that indicates that more time is needed at this level. If they show limited progress, then a more intense and frequent support model might be needed. The team might decide at this point to recommend Rachel and the other student for Tier 2 instruction.

Isn't that what we want for our students—to have them leave the classroom satisfied? That is the purpose of RTI: to meet students' needs in order to increase their academic achievement. It's all in the planning and preparation. Once you research a list of instructional practices that work (much like the cook who locates appropriate recipes), you spend the rest of your teaching time attending to the ways that your students respond to that instruction. Are students learning? How do you know? How can you modify your teaching to help your students meet with success? The strategies in this book can help you achieve the goals you have for your students without a lot of advance preparation and within a reasonable amount of time. In addition, they can help you make a smooth transition from Tier 1 to Tier 2 instruction with students.

Tier 1: At this level, all students are learning within the whole-class setting from a highly qualified teacher who implements evidence-based, high-quality core instruction. This type of instruction can take the form of the general education teacher being "on stage" as students listen, take notes, or follow his or her words and actions. The danger of this type of instruction is that, too often, students are passively taking in information, and therefore they are not really attaching meaning to the content and internalizing it. Tier 1 can, however, include cooperative-learning groups in which the teacher skillfully balances this potentially passive student learning with small groups within the whole-class setting.

Note that all the research-based strategies contained in this book may be used during a Tier 1 phase of instruction because they can help you organize the learning environment to meet the diverse needs of your students. And let's face it, in any classroom (or in any place where there are groups of people), there are individuals with diverse interests and needs. So approaching Tier 1 instruction in a way that acknowledges that you have a class full of individuals with different needs just makes sense, and the strategies in this book can address those basic needs.

Making a smooth transition to Tier 2: When you look at students' work as evidence of their abilities and rate of progress within the Tier 1 phase, you are likely to identify some students who need additional time for practice and reteaching. This is the time to move those students to Tier 2 and to kick the intensity of their instruction up a notch. Research indicates that a large percentage of students who receive Tier 2 instruction succeed and return to Tier 1 without any further instructional support.

The list below shows how instruction intensifies in Tier 2.

- Tier 2 is supplemental to the high-quality, core, whole-class instruction.
- Instruction happens in small groups with the teacher focusing on specific skills to teach individual students. For example, if a student is showing difficulty decoding unfamiliar words in ways that hinder his or her ability to keep up with whole-class reading, then you would implement specific strategies to guide his or her decoding and use of context clues.
- Student progress is monitored every two weeks in simple, systematic ways (see pages 44–46 on progress monitoring).
- Instruction is refocused to meet the specific needs of students.

The Intention and Significance of Tier 2 Instruction

Tier 2 instruction is designed to supplement, not supplant, Tier 1 instruction. The premise is to ramp up the intensity of instruction by preteaching or reteaching targeted skills a student needs to learn successfully within Tier 1 instruction. Tier 2 is part of the cycle of good instruction that includes whatever support the student requires to be successful. Again, in this cycle, every student receives Tier 1 instruction.

THE TEACHER AS DECISION MAKER

In order for students to move seamlessly from Tier 1 to Tier 2, we need to make sure that we are making the best instructional decisions to guide the learning process. It would be a tedious job to actually stop and count up all the decisions one teacher makes in a single day. Our decisions affect not only the present moment, but also may affect a child's life well into the future. For example, your classroom-management decisions about desk arrangement, seating charts, and basic classroom routines affect your students while they are in your classroom. The decisions you make about what to teach, how to teach, and how to assess learning, on the other hand, have consequences that may extend far beyond the time these students are in your classroom. Just think about it—students' learning builds upon prior learning from grade to grade. If students are not receiving content-area information in ways that they can connect with and that meet their individual needs, their academic performance will suffer as they try to fill in the gaps when they move to the next grade. The bottom-line question to ask yourself is, "Do my instructional and assessment decisions match the learners in my classroom?" The answer will probably be yes. Most students find ways to connect to a teacher's style and to the content being taught. However, certain students need additional methods of instruction and supports to guide them to make meaningful connections between a teacher's instruction and their learning.

Let's look at two classrooms in which fifth-grade teachers are providing reading instruction to their classes.

Mr. Pell's Class: Mr. Pell introduces a book about butterflies and reads aloud the title and the author's name. He gives students a few minutes to look over the text. Mr. Pell values the thoughts of his students, so he asks them if they have any questions. When no one responds, Mr. Pell asks more specifically if anyone came across any difficult vocabulary words. One student raises his hand and offers a word, and Mr. Pell reviews the word with the class. Satisfied that students are ready to move on, he instructs them to get together with their reading partners and begin to read the text. Afterward, students respond to comprehension questions. As Mr. Pell collects the responses, he looks around the room, feeling pleased with the outcome of the lesson. But when he grades the responses, Mr. Pell finds that nine of his 23 students have failed.

Mr. Knight's Class: Next door, Mr. Knight is introducing the same lesson on butterflies. He begins the lesson by having students make predictions about the text they are about to read. Mr. Knight has prepared five vocabulary words that he thinks are important to know and that may be challenging for students, and he reviews these words using visual reinforcement. Mr. Knight then leads a brief discussion to activate students' prior knowledge of the topic. He knows which students require additional visual supports to organize their thinking, so he encourages them to complete a graphic organizer to guide their thoughts about the topic before they begin to read. Mr. Knight models the graphic organizer at the front of the class as a whole-class discussion unfolds. Following the class discussion, Mr. Knight has some students read in pairs, some independently, and a few students read with him at the back table. The way Mr. Knight structures this reading time allows him to implement strategic reading instruction to the students he knows will require direct instruction. He places those students who need some support in a partner reading—a peer collaborative— experience, and he encourages those students who do not need additional support to read independently. Following the lesson, students answer comprehension questions. When Mr. Knight grades the responses, he finds that only one out of 24 students has failed.

Which teacher would you like to be: Mr. Pell or Mr. Knight? Both teachers demonstrated a sense of caring about the success of their students, but it's clear that Mr. Knight demonstrates the value of instructional decisions as it connects to student success.

It is evident that the daily decisions we teachers make will shape the attitude and performance of our students. In order to be effective decision makers, we must turn toward reflective teaching practices. The RTI framework can help any teacher become more reflective and better equipped to make the best decisions for his or her students.

REFLECTIVE TEACHING

As we think about the value of our instructional decisions and awareness of students' needs, we begin to strengthen our ability to be reflective teachers. Reflective thinking is all about reviewing our current teaching practices and linking them to prior instructional experiences in order to promote more effective teaching practices. A reflective teacher becomes determined to make the best instructional decisions. In 1983, Donald Schon introduced reflective practice in *The Reflective Practitioner*. Schon was inspired by the work of John Dewey (1933), who suggested that reflection begins with a dilemma. Dewey believed that effective teachers refrained from drawing conclusions about a dilemma until they gathered enough information, analyzed the problem, gained new knowledge, and then came to a well-informed decision. This process of careful contemplation is exactly what brings about new learning, and it can guide us to make informed instructional decisions.

Let's look at how two teachers approach a similar dilemma.

Mrs. Smith's Dilemma: *Kyle is a third-grade student who is struggling to keep up with his peers in reading. Kyle's teacher, Mrs. Smith, monitors him by listening in and observing his performance. After two weeks, Mrs. Smith analyzes her anecdotal notes and concludes that Kyle is definitely struggling to apply the reading skills she has taught during whole-class instructional time. Kyle's grades in other academic areas are at grade level, but Mrs. Smith determines that he struggles when asked to read independently, so she decides to mention this to her instructional support team for further discussion and problem solving. At the meeting, when asked why she is concerned about Kyle, Mrs. Smith replies, "I just know." She supports her statement by handing out copies of her anecdotal notes and says, "Isn't it obvious?"*

Mrs. Brinkman's Dilemma: *Another third-grade teacher, Mrs. Brinkman, has the same dilemma with one of her students, Luke. Like Mrs. Smith, she jots down anecdotal notes to support her observations. In addition, she creates some simple skill assessments that she administers to Luke as the rest of the class is reading in groups. These assessments provide information on Luke's ability to decode and comprehend text presented as sentences or in paragraphs. During these quick skill assessments Mrs. Brinkman also gathers data on how Luke applies active reading strategies. She compares her notes with the results of the skill assessments, providing her with evidence that Luke is only able to connect to text at a literal level. He does not stop to monitor his comprehension and often skips unfamiliar vocabulary words. He has great difficulty determining importance when reading, as evidenced by his retelling irrelevant information and missing key facts to summarize what he has read. A quick decoding assessment shows that Luke has strong decoding skills, but he is not using context clues to construct meaning from unfamiliar words as he reads. So he just keeps reading without trying to figure out what words mean. In a meeting with her support team, when Mrs. Brinkman is asked why she is concerned about Luke, she shares her anecdotal notes, along with results of her skill assessments. In addition, she shares her instructional strategies log, which outlines all of the interventions she has implemented with Luke so far. The data Mrs. Brinkman has collected over time confirms her instincts that this student needs additional instructional support.*

Which teacher would you like to be? They both demonstrated clear insights and instincts. Both of them observed, analyzed, and went through the proper channels to get support. Mrs. Brinkman, however, gathered specific data based on clear evidence of instructional decisions to support her student's progress. Mrs. Brinkman was able to analyze the data she collected in ways that helped her to gain new knowledge and that justified her instincts that Luke needed additional instructional support. Mrs. Brinkman is a natural when it comes to working within a Response to Intervention mindset.

Donald Schon asserts that teachers must think on their feet by applying previous experiences to new situations. We can make decisions about situations in the present based on what we know has worked in past situations. We can make the most of the power of our decisions by thinking in new ways about problems we have solved in the past. What sets great teachers apart from good ones is the ability to be comfortable with uncertainty. Great teachers have the ability to create a learning environment that has a free-flowing feeling. These teachers plan thoughtfully. They implement their lessons reflectively in the moments of teaching and are ready to make any necessary instructional decisions for specific students. Successful reflective teachers are flexible and open to change, challenge, and innovation. They realize that their instructional decisions may serve as the path to students' frustration or as the key to their success.

The following checklists will help you become a more reflective teacher:

- The Reflective Teacher's General Checklist on page 127 can help you make effective instructional decisions as you plan, implement, and assess your instruction and its alignment with students' performance.

- The Lesson Reflection Checklist on page 128 can guide your thinking following a lesson.

Chapter 2

RTI in the 21st-Century Classroom

No two learners are alike, but Donovan and Bransford (2005) outlined the principles of learning in the 21st century and found that learners in today's classrooms share the following characteristics:

- *Students come to the classroom with prior knowledge and experiences:* Teachers must activate this prior understanding by building upon students' background knowledge in order to promote new learning.

- *Students create deeper understandings by applying a strong factual and conceptual knowledge base to real-world contexts:* Teachers must guide students to make meaningful connections by modeling their own thinking as well as by asking questions to guide higher-level thinking.

- *Students are aware of how they learn best and how to monitor and reflect on their learning:* Teachers must provide opportunities for students to regulate their own learning, and they must dedicate time to guiding students to create optimal learning habits. One way to accomplish this goal is by presenting information through multiple representations—visual, auditory, as well as through cooperative-learning activities. Teachers should also give students time to reflect on what they have learned through group discussions and/or short written reflections (Darling-Hammond & Bransford 2005).

The new Common Core State Standards (CCSS) for literacy push for students' reading, writing, speaking, and listening skills to be at a level that prepares them for college and a successful life beyond it. The standards are designed to be robust and relevant to the real world. The reasoning is that the better prepared our American students are, the better prepared our communities will be to compete successfully in the global economy. (For more information on CCSS, visit www.corestandards.org). Aligning the standards, curriculum, evidence-based teaching practices, and students' needs is a major challenge, to be sure, but Response to Intervention is a natural fit that can help you create a positive and productive learning environment.

Setting Up for Success: The Reading Workshop Approach

You have a lot to think about as you set up a learning environment. A reading workshop approach has the structure and flexibility you need to guide diverse learners, while allowing you to balance instructional responsibilities within an RTI framework.

Here's a model of the reading workshop approach in one third-grade classroom:

Mrs. Hall has just taught a mini-lesson on writing a reading response letter. In the two weeks leading up to the mini-lesson, she has become aware of which of her students need additional support. She also knows which students would benefit from peer collaboration, as well as those who just need time to read independently to complete the day's reading tasks. Mrs. Hall knows all this because she has observed all of her students, taken anecdotal notes, interviewed them about their feelings about reading, analyzed their reading notebooks, and monitored their comprehension and vocabulary skills through classroom assessments. Using this collection of data, Mrs. Hall made the following schedule, based on the specific needs of her students.

- **Small Group With Teacher Support:** Mrs. Hall provides direct instruction on a targeted skill to three students at the back table. She notices that these students had written basic summaries instead of a genuine response to the reading. To move them beyond the rote retelling of events, she knows she has to model the process of making meaningful predictions and connections while reading. Mrs. Hall guides students to make reading an active process that goes beyond merely summarizing.

- **Small Group:** Mrs. Hall asks some students to work collaboratively in groups of three to five to discuss a book they are reading.

- **Pairs:** Mrs. Hall has some students work in pairs to support deeper levels of comprehension by discussing their connections and predictions, and sharing new vocabulary words they learned through their reading.

- **Independent Reading:** Mrs. Hall tells some students to read independently to identify the sequence of events along with their connections and thoughts about those events.

Each student is busy reading, responding, and applying active reading strategies. Each student receives the necessary support to reach deeper levels of comprehension.

RTI and the Workshop Approach

Reading instruction in grades 3 and up usually includes instruction in vocabulary, fluency, and comprehension. As the curriculum becomes more concentrated, students begin to learn about the facts in the content areas in greater depth. Students begin to move from learning to read to reading to learn. The Fountas and Pinnell (2001) reading workshop model blends perfectly with instruction within Tier 1 and Tier 2 of the RTI framework. This workshop model is a natural fit for several reasons. For one, it is a model of instruction that is already being utilized in classrooms nationwide. It also enables teachers to provide effective instruction to a whole class or small groups.

While Fountas and Pinnell advocate a 60-minute reading workshop in an elementary classroom, any phase of instruction can be adjusted to meet time constraints. Here's the general outline of a reading workshop lesson.

The Whole-Class Mini-Lesson *(5–15 minutes)*

- All students observe as you demonstrate a particular skill or strategy.

- You may gradually encourage students to interact following the demonstration.

Small-Group Instruction/Peer Collaboration/Independent Work *(15–25 minutes)*

- You assign independent and group activities so students can apply the focus of the mini-lesson to their own reading.

- This time is an invaluable feature of Tier 2 instruction because you are free to work with small groups of students while others read independently or meet in groups for book discussions.

Whole-Class Share and Evaluation *(5–10 minutes)*

- During whole-class sharing time, you and students come back together to review what they have learned.

The Whole-Class Mini-Lesson

The mini-lesson launches the reading instruction for the day. It begins with a teacher demonstration of a particular strategy, skill, or idea. Fountas and Pinnell (2001) group mini-lessons into three categories:

1. Lessons on management (including classroom routines to help the workshop model run smoothly)

2. Lessons on strategies and skills (including the mental moves that successful readers use to construct meaning from text)

3. Lessons on literary analysis (including reading closely to analyze text themes and structures)

In this phase, you model your thinking to show what you would like your students to learn that day. You set the stage for students to gradually take responsibility for independently applying the skills and strategies that successful readers use every time they read.

Each mini-lesson covers one of the essential elements students will need to become successful readers. Teachers decide which skill or strategy to teach during this phase by aligning standards, curriculum, and a knowledge of what kind of support their students need. They also base some of their decisions about what to teach on the data they collect from their observations and student work. (For more information on assessment, see Chapter 3).

Typically, students who are struggling do not have a clear sense of how to construct meaning from text in meaningful ways. These are the students who would need Tier 2 instruction in order to guide them to successfully read independently.

ACTIVE READING STRATEGIES: TEACHING READERS THE LANGUAGE OF THINKING

The words of a text alone are not enough for deep comprehension to take place; what the reader does with the words is what creates meaning.

The rich research on reading comprehension dating back to the mid-70s provides us with deep knowledge of what good readers do when they read. Among those researchers are Duke and Pearson (2002), who found that good readers do the following:

- Read actively
- Set clear goals and constantly evaluate whether the text and their understanding meet these goals
- Preview the text before they read, noting structure and text sections that may be relevant to meeting their goals

- Make predictions as they read
- Make decisions about what's important to read, what to reread, what not to read, and so on
- Construct, revise, and question the meanings they create as they read
- Try to determine the meaning of unfamiliar words and ideas
- Integrate their prior knowledge with the information in the text
- Think about the author's purpose
- Monitor their understanding, making adjustments as necessary
- Respond to the text intellectually and emotionally
- Adjust their thinking and strategy use according to different kinds of texts
- Pay close attention to the setting and characters in narrative texts
- Summarize key points in expository texts
- Process text before, during, and after they read
- Take short breaks as they read to strengthen their ability to process text and monitor their understanding

We know that comprehension is a consuming, continuous, and complex activity that good readers find rewarding and productive. There are varying opinions among researchers about which active reading strategies are the most important, but most agree that the following seven strategies outlined by Harvey and Goudvis (2007) describe the foundation of what active readers do.

Activate Background Knowledge (Schema)

- Think about prior knowledge
- Connect new information to known information and use this connection to deepen comprehension
- Merge thinking with new learning

Ask Questions

- Wonder about the content and big ideas
- Question the author
- Read to discover answers and gain information
- Do further research to answer questions not answered in text

Draw Inferences

- Use context clues to figure out the meaning of unfamiliar words and ideas
- Use text evidence and schema to draw conclusions

Determine Importance

- Focus on key information and code the text to deepen understanding
- Distinguish between what you think is important and what the author intends readers to grasp

Visualize

- Create interpretations based on text evidence
- Create images and use all senses to "feel" the words and ideas

Clarify

- Listen to an inner voice while creating a conversation with the text
- Notice when meaning breaks down
- Leave "thinking tracks" by jotting down thoughts
- Stop, think, and respond to information
- Implement strategies to restore and create understanding, such as reread for clarification; read on to construct meaning; use context to break down unfamiliar words or ideas; skip difficult parts and continue to see if meaning becomes clear, then go back to reread to check for understanding while thinking about the text evidence and what makes sense

Synthesize

- Paraphrase information
- Move from facts to ideas by combining text evidence with other ideas from the text and/or from background knowledge
- Revise thinking as more text evidence unfolds; rethink ideas and opinions
- Generate knowledge; merge what is known with new information to form a new idea or perspective

These reading strategies serve as flexible tools for guiding comprehension, empowering students to tackle challenging texts with greater independence.

BALANCED COMPREHENSION INSTRUCTION

Effective comprehension instruction requires that you balance your explicit instruction with sufficient time for students to apply the strategies in their writing and in group discussions. It also requires a supportive classroom environment and a structured model to deepen instruction.

A Supportive Classroom Context

Duke and Pearson (2002) argue that good instruction is not enough. They say the following features must be in place in order for comprehension instruction to be effective:

- Students must spend a great deal of time reading.
- Students must read real texts for real reasons.
- Students must be familiar with the range of text genres they are expected to comprehend.
- Students must be surrounded by an environment rich in literacy, one that promotes vocabulary and concept development through well-chosen texts and, above all, discussion of words and their meanings.
- Students must have ample experience writing texts for others to read.

A Model of Comprehension Instruction Within a Reading Workshop Approach

Duke and Pearson believe that the most effective comprehension instruction must provide opportunities for students to integrate their reading, writing, listening, and speaking skills. This model of comprehension may help you plan within the reading workshop model. It includes the following five components:

1. The teacher provides an explicit description of the strategy, including when and how the strategy should be used.
2. The teacher and/or a student models the strategy in action.
3. The teacher plans for collaborative use of the strategy in action between students, with his or her support.
4. The teacher provides guided practice using the strategy with gradual release of responsibility, leading students toward independent use.
5. The teacher allows time for students to apply the strategy independently; the teacher supports students through guided practice until they are ready to apply the strategy independently.

Peer Collaboration and Independent Work

In this phase of the reading workshop, most students have shown that they are ready to apply certain skills and strategies. This is a good time for students to practice reading silently, complete vocabulary skill work, or discuss books with peers.

Whole-Class Share and Evaluation

At the conclusion of the reading workshop time, the teacher guides a whole-class discussion in which students share their thinking about their reading and strategy use during workshop time. This is also a good time for students to evaluate their own learning and strategy use—not to mention a good opportunity for you to assess what students have learned (see anecdotal notes and checklists in Chapter 3).

Differentiating Instruction Within the RTI Tiers

Today's teachers are faced with the reality of teaching students of diverse backgrounds, abilities, and interests. We must teach the core content and skills that all students must learn and be able to utilize, but let's face it—teachers who take a one-size-fits-all approach are leaving a lot of learning to chance. Students need teachers who hold high expectations but who also provide support when it is needed. Within the reading workshop structure, you can easily differentiate whole-class mini-lessons, small-group assignments, and independent learning experiences to support your students' needs. In fact, it is clear that RTI and differentiated instruction share a common premise: Effective teaching is responsive teaching. And in order for our teaching to be responsive, we must make the time to notice what each of our students requires. We must be able to look at the whole group not as one mass blur but as a collection of individuals. We must make certain that we notice who is learning and who needs additional support. Since RTI requires teachers to be able to provide varying levels of support to targeted groups of students, the model of differentiating instruction is a natural fit. When speaking about differentiating instruction, Carol Ann Tomlinson (1999) states, "Children already come to us differentiated. It just makes sense that we would differentiate our instruction in response to them."

WHAT DIFFERENTIATED INSTRUCTION IS

According to Tomlinson and Edison (2003), a variety of components makes differentiated instruction effective. Teachers who differentiate instruction begin with clear learning goals for their students. These goals are linked to best practices and effective assessment so teachers know how well students understand what is being taught. Instruction occurs as teachers flexibly arrange students to learn as a group, in pairs, and individually. The learning environment guides students to share in the responsibility for their learning. When teachers differentiate instruction, they plan instructional methodologies that fit the strengths and needs of their students.

USING DIFFERENTIATED INSTRUCTION WITH RTI

The essential tenets of RTI connect seamlessly with differentiation. In fact, RTI can only be successful when teachers differentiate instruction, because both focus squarely on each student's individual strengths and needs. Both seek to provide students with a variety of options for taking information in, making sense of ideas, and expressing what they have learned. This chart shows how differentiation connects with RTI.

	Differentiated Instruction	RTI
The premise is that all students can learn, and if they are not learning, it is the teacher's responsibility to identify and apply effective instructional techniques to guide them to success.	✓	✓
There is a strong connection between instructional methods and students' learning.	✓	✓
Struggling students are identified early in order to proactively guide them to achieve.	✓	✓
Instructional strategies are research-based.	✓	✓
Students' progress is monitored and analyzed so teachers can make wise instructional decisions.	✓	✓
Teachers collaborate with colleagues to problem solve and determine the most appropriate instructional interventions for students.	✓	✓

LINKING RTI AND DIFFERENTIATION

The process of instruction within the RTI framework strongly mirrors the intentional teaching entailed in differentiating instruction. One difference is that RTI includes more frequent assessments through progress monitoring. (See Chapter 3 for an in-depth discussion of assessment.)

Generally, there are some key steps you can take to forge a smooth connection between differentiating instruction and following an RTI framework:

Define the instructional focus:

- *What is the student's learning problem?*
- *What are the academic goals for the student?*
- *What examples of a student's work do I have that demonstrate that he or she is struggling with a specific learning problem?*

Develop an action plan:

- *Which research-based strategies would be helpful for this student?*
- *How might I differentiate instruction for this student?*
- *How long will I implement this intervention before assessing the student's progress?*

Implement the action plan:

- *Check for fidelity of instruction: Is the instruction being implemented appropriately, consistently, and completely?*
- *Do the student's performance and work samples indicate that the intervention is effective? Collect the student's work samples as evidence of his or her performance.*
- *What instructional adjustments need to be made? Is the student responding positively to instruction? Does the student's performance indicate that he or she is learning and making progress?*

Evaluate the effectiveness of instruction and student learning:

- *What does my collected data (student work samples, tests, anecdotal notes) tell me about the student's response to my instructional strategies?*
- *Do I need to further differentiate instruction for this student? Do I need to create a new instructional action plan?*

OPTIONS FOR DIFFERENTIATING INSTRUCTION

In planning how to differentiate instruction, I find it a great comfort that there are so many options available. Discussed below are four options that Carol Ann Tomlinson (2001) suggests.

1. **Differentiate by Varying Types of Questions**

   Varying the types of questions you ask allows you to set students up for success as you shape their thinking to reach deeper levels of understanding. You can vary the complexity of the thinking students need to do to answer the questions. For example, you might weave in recall questions (*who, what, where,* and *when* questions) that foster the ability to comprehend on a literal level. Finding the answer to such questions often requires the simple stating of a fact. And when students are ready, you can ask questions that require them to evaluate and apply their knowledge. For example, asking students to express an opinion based on facts from a text encourages them to read in meaningful and active ways. (See Bloom's Taxonomy for further discussion on varying question types.)

2. **Differentiate by Providing Various Opportunities for Student Engagement**
Engaging lessons motivate students to put forth their best efforts. Sustaining student engagement allows you to address their learning needs and notice which strategies work for certain students, as well as how deeply they understand the content. When you offer a variety of opportunities for students to become engaged, you are allowing each student to construct meaning from the content through multiple pathways.

3. **Differentiate by Creating Flexible Learning Groups**
Types of groups include the following:

- Whole group
- Small groups of varying degrees of readiness (heterogeneous)
- Small groups of like readiness (homogeneous)
- Independent or individual work

4. **Differentiate Instruction Through Ongoing Assessment**
In addition to traditional forms of assessment, you should incorporate authentic and performance-based, or formative, assessments. These assessments give you a sense of how well a student is learning, and you can plan future lessons based on what you learn from your student's performance. The more you incorporate performance assessments, the more you can differentiate your instruction to meet the learning needs of specific students. When you think about how to maximize your instruction by incorporating ongoing assessments, you should consider including the following elements:

- Assess students' sense of the subject before, during, and after instruction.
- Include a pre-assessment in order to determine students' prior knowledge base.
- Implement formative assessments to track students' progress through-out the learning process, as well as to allow students to track their own progress.
- Incorporate summative assessments so you and your students can assess whether learning goals have been reached—and to decide on the upcoming steps.

Differentiating Tier 1 Instruction in the Reading Workshop

The goal of leveled assignments is to provide a better instructional match with the individual needs of students within a whole-class setting. Assignments for Tier 1 in the reading workshop model may be leveled according to a differentiated learning framework that you develop based on careful observation and diagnosis of students' individual strengths and needs. It is your decision whether students complete leveled assignments individually, with a partner, or in a collaborative learning experience. In order to make assignments meaningful, you must align curriculum, standards, and any Individualized Education Program (IEP) goals students may have. You can use the following six ways to structure leveled assignments for Tier 1:

1. **Challenge Level:** Bloom's Taxonomy is a useful guide to differentiate students according to their abilities and to deepen their skills at various levels of thinking (Anderson & Krathwohl 2001). For example, when teaching about the solar system, you could create leveled questions that demonstrate various depths of thinking. One question could ask students to list the planets (requiring the recollection of facts), while another question could ask students to compare Saturn and Jupiter (requiring synthesis and analysis of key ideas). (For more information on Bloom's Taxonomy and a reproducible, visit www.scholastic.com/teachers/article/elements-differentiation-blooms-taxonomy.)

2. **Complexity:** When you differentiate by complexity, you address the needs of students at introductory levels, as well as those who are ready for more abstract, higher-level thinking. You can usually plan for your organization at the following three levels:

   - Least complex
   - More complex
   - Most complex

3. **Resources:** Matching resources to students' specific instructional needs or readiness is known as "layering resources."

4. **Outcome:** Students using the same materials often yield different outcomes. Some students can operate at advanced levels of thinking and learn to apply that learning, while others can work within a different framework that limits their frustration but still offers a challenge. To layer assignments by differentiated outcomes, you must have a clear understanding of your students' readiness. To organize your planning, you may think in terms of a basic task and an advanced task for each expected outcome.

5. **Process:** You may want your students to reach similar outcomes but to use different processes to get there. You may assign a basic task to one group

Recommendations for Deciding When and How to Level an Assignment

Level by Challenge/Complexity When . . .

some students need more time to work on content or a skill and other students are ready for more advanced work. For example, you could have one group work on recalling or paraphrasing key points of a text, while another group is analyzing the same text but also taking it a step further by identifying themes in common with another previously read text.

Level by Resources When . . .

there is an activity in which varied resources could be matched with students' needs and readiness. For example, give one group chart paper and colored pencils, another group an audio recorder, and another group access to a computer. Have each group be responsible for discussing a specific aspect of the text. The first group would create a visual graphic, the second group would use verbal skills, and the third group would use written expression to meet the requirements of the task.

Level by Outcome When . . .

there is an activity in which the same materials could be used to work on both basic and more advanced outcomes. This method works when tasks have more than one correct answer, so students have the opportunity to respond. While all students in the group use the same task and/or material, differentiation occurs by letting individuals answer at their own levels of ability, thereby yielding different outcomes from the same task.

Level by Process When . . .

there is an activity in which students could benefit from working on the same outcome but doing different kinds of work. For example, assign all students the task of reading a short text and then writing a summary of it. One group could partner-read by taking turns reading and listening to one another. One group could actively listen as the text is read to them. Another group could read silently. Following the reading, each student writes a short summary of the text.

Level by Product When . . .

there is an activity that could result in more than one way for students to show what they have learned. For example, as you read aloud a story to your class, require each student to take notes on the text and then present a short summary of the main idea. Some students could present their notes and summary by sketching the ideas. Other students could use an outline and a short paragraph, while others may list important words from the text and then prepare a brief oral presentation to summarize the main idea.

and an advanced task to another group. For example, you might assign the same research project to two groups but ask one group to use more advanced research processes.

6. **Product:** You may form groups based on learning preferences, allowing for students to exhibit their understanding through various pathways. For example, you may offer students the choice of responding orally or through written expression.

Moving Along the Continuum of Comprehension

One of the overall goals of RTI is to help students reach deeper levels of comprehension. As we differentiate and plan instruction to meet individual needs, we must guide students along a continuum of comprehension strategies through meaningful reading experiences. For students in grades 3–5, we need to provide a lot of time to practice these active reading skills by reading a variety of texts—and reading often. You can provide this practice within the structure of your lessons.

According to Harvey and Daniels (2009), successful readers move along the following continuum as they develop deeper levels of comprehension:

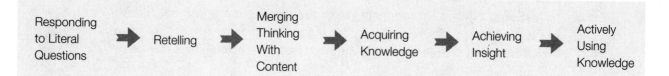

Responding to Literal Questions → Retelling → Merging Thinking With Content → Acquiring Knowledge → Achieving Insight → Actively Using Knowledge

Responding to Literal Questions: This is the most basic level of comprehension. It demonstrates readers' ability to skim and locate key words in the text that match the question, but it does not demonstrate their ability to paraphrase or gain deeper understanding.

Retelling: Readers who can retell the events of a story show the ability to put thoughts together sequentially. Retelling also demonstrates readers' ability to remember the basic order of events, but it does not demonstrate deeper understanding.

Merging Thinking With Content: Deeper understanding begins to take root when readers begin to combine their thinking and background knowledge with the content. Deeper levels of comprehension begin at this level.

Acquiring Knowledge: Readers acquire new knowledge as they combine prior knowledge with new information.

Achieving Insight: Readers produce new ideas as they combine prior knowledge with new knowledge.

Actively Using Knowledge: Readers gain new insights and understandings and begin to actively connect and apply these new ideas to their daily experiences.

Chapters 4–6 are filled with research-based strategies that will provide students with instruction that does the following:

- Familiarizes them with the structure of narrative and expository text

- Targets the development of content-area vocabulary

- Builds reading fluency

- Teaches them how, why, when, and where to use a variety of comprehension strategies

Engage Every Student With Strategies That Motivate

As you strive to guide students' learning within an RTI framework, you must consider their level of engagement. Student engagement is vital to the degree of their response to instruction. When you consistently use engaging instructional strategies and classroom practices, students are able to do the following:

- Take more responsibility for their own learning and record and assess their progress

- Develop better habits of learning that increase personal efficacy, self-discipline, social efficacy, and group-participation skills

- Assess how coursework links to personal learning goals and their future aspirations

- Make connections between effort and achievement

- Make better decisions regarding time- and task-management

- Use group cooperation and team-building skills to work more productively with classmates

- Use a 21st-century skill set (such as inquiry, problem solving, and critical thinking) to complete work that is both important and meaningful

EVERY-STUDENT-RESPONDS STRATEGIES

When you encourage all students to be active in the learning process, there is a better chance for learning to take place. Again, as you plan for effective instruction within an RTI framework, remember that student engagement is a strong link to successful outcomes. Students who are engaged are students who are attaching personal meaning to what they're learning and, therefore, have a better chance of responding positively to instruction. In addition, when you include response modes to engage students, you are helping them develop their critical-thinking skills. Here are a few simple but effective ways to engage students during Tier 1 and Tier 2 instruction.

Thumbs Up, Down, Sideways

During reading workshop, intermittently ask students to make a judgment based on what someone else has said or read. Then ask the rest of the class to indicate agreement with a thumbs-up or disagreement with a thumbs-down. If students are unsure, they can turn their thumbs sideways. And remember, have students explain why they agree, disagree, or are uncertain; students must justify their thinking—that is the essence of helping them develop higher-level thinking and deeper understanding.

Whiteboard Response

Materials: *whiteboard, marker, eraser for each student*

Give each student his or her own dry-erase board, marker, and eraser. Have everyone respond to specific questions and hold up his or her board for discussion.

Fingers Under Chin

This is a nice, discreet way to have students respond—it's great for hesitant participants. Place a value and attach a meaning to students' holding a certain number of fingers under their chin in response to questions. For example, you might say: "Hold one finger under your chin if you agree, two if you disagree." You can also have students use this method to show their answer to a multiple-choice question: "Hold one finger under your chin for A, two for B, three for C, and four for D."

Hold Up a Shape

Materials: *shapes template, white or colored paper, scissors*

This activity takes a little bit of prep work, but once you've done it, you are set for the rest of the year. Cut out shapes, such as squares, circles, rectangles, octagons (all similar in size) and laminate them. You can also cut out different colors of the same shape. Before you begin a group discussion, hand a set of different shapes or different colors of the same shape to each student. Use the same process as the Fingers Under the Chin activity: "Hold up a circle if you agree, a square if you disagree, or an octagon if you're uncertain." "Hold up a blue circle if you agree, a green circle if you disagree, or a yellow circle if you're uncertain."

Palm Up, Palm Down

This is another great strategy for timid learners, in which students place their palms up if they agree and down if they disagree. You can also have students place their palms up if they feel comfortable about responding and their palms down if they would rather not be called on to share.

Choice Cards

Materials: *index cards, markers*

After students listen to or read a passage, use choice cards to encourage conversation and independent thinking. You can tailor choice cards to the specific type of question you want to ask; for example, if you use a nonfiction passage to review content-area material, "True-False," or "Yes-No" cards should do the trick. For a study of genre, you could use "Fact-Fiction" cards, and so on.

Whole-Body Response

This quick-response mode gets students up and moving; it works well when you notice students passively sitting in their seats. Movement can increase students' alertness when important learning is happening. Although you have the flexibility to assign a movement to a particular response, here are a few examples:

Stand up if it's true.
Sit down if it's false.
Step forward if it's true.
Step backward if it's false.

Hit the Buzzer

Materials: *colored paper, scissors*

This engagement requires a little initial preparation. Laminate enough circles for a small group [using yellow circles of the same size works well, but you can use any color(s) you like]. Tell students to place the circles on their desk or table and explain that the circles are "buzzers" that they will hit to respond to a question. Throughout your group discussion and reading review, say, "Get your buzzers ready." Even the most unmotivated students sit up straight, eager to be the first to hit the buzzer. When you ask a question based on the group's reading or content-area material, students respond based on who hits their buzzer first, next, and so forth. In order to keep a natural flow to the instructional and discussion time, you may have students tally each time they hit their buzzer to respond.

Think-Pair-Share

This is a tried-and-true method to encourage independent thinking while students collaborate and learn from others. In response to a reading or topic of discussion, students formulate their own thoughts and then share them with a peer. Pairs take turns listening and sharing as they deepen their own personal ideas and gain the perspective of a peer.

Think-Pair-Square-Share

This is Think-Pair-Share with a twist. Follow the steps in Think-Pair-Share and then have one pair share with another pair—hence, the square.

Creating a Strategic Learning Environment During Tier 2 Instruction

One focus of Tier 2 instruction is to make students aware of the steps involved in successful learning. They need to know what is required of them in order for learning to take place. Breaking down the learning tasks into strategic steps enables struggling learners to organize their thinking in order to achieve their goals. Students learn best when they are free to explore and gain knowledge through active learning and visual imagery (Marzano 2003). They also need time in class to apply a variety of metacognitive strategies such as self-monitoring and self-reflecting. A main goal of Tier 2 instruction is to guide students to become independent, strategic thinkers.

Use the following classroom-based structures during Tier 2 instruction to enable students to generalize strategies when they are in the whole-class setting.

STRATEGIES IN ACTION DISPLAY

Dedicate one wall in the classroom to displaying examples of students' strategies in action. The important thing is to ensure that the strategies are prominently displayed. This way, students have a daily visual reminder of effective reading strategies that they can use throughout the day, regardless of the setting. You can simply display a brief description of each strategy along with some student samples that show the how the strategy is used. You can also display students' descriptions of how a particular strategy helped them understand a text.

STRATEGY SHARE DISCUSSIONS

In addition to daily discussion, you can initiate a weekly discussion time to allow students to share what they have noticed about their strategy use. Tier 2 students can learn from other students and gain insight into their own strategic thinking.

STRATEGY PRACTICE LABS

Students need to understand that one strategy may be used across genres and subject-area reading. You can set up weekly strategy labs to help students apply a specific strategy to specific genres and content. These labs provide time for them to internalize why a certain strategy works best with certain content material and genres. A typical strategy lab session includes time for a brief reteaching or review of a strategy. Students then have the opportunity to apply the strategy while you monitor how they use it independently. You should plan carefully to include a different content-area text and/or genre each time students participate in the strategy lab, so they can see the versatility of strategies. This strategy lab time can help create flexible, strategic readers.

MODEL, MODEL, MODEL

Keep in mind that students need to see strategies in action in order to be able to apply them effectively. Continue to model as you encourage students who are applying a strategy successfully to show what they know.

Tier 2 Interventions: Making the Most of Small-Group Instructional Time

The purpose of Tier 2 instruction is to provide additional support for students whose classroom performance has demonstrated the need for reteaching of concepts and content. Tier 2 small-group instruction is only effective when it is directly linked to the curriculum. Instruction is structured, systematic, and scaffolded in a way that leads students toward independence. Model your thinking and your application of active reading strategies. Teach students to become aware of their own thinking processes (metacognitive awareness) through explicit teacher modeling, while sharing what you are thinking; for example, "David, I noticed you stopped reading and then you went back to reread the previous page. Did that help clarify what you were confused about?" As you tell students what you notice, they become aware of their strengths and the gaps in their knowledge. Create a positive learning environment while encouraging effort and a positive work ethic; for example by saying something like, "Maria, great thinking. You just demonstrated that you are able to use context clues to figure out an unfamiliar word." Make sure to allow time for students to discuss how using a particular strategy helped them understand what they read. This reflection time can go a long way in leading them toward applying skills in the future.

Setting Up Tier 2 Small-Group Instruction: A Sample

Tier 2 instruction varies depending on the individual learning needs of students, but the basic structure is always the same. It is important to maintain a consistent structure: A predictable structure ushers students toward applying the strategies on their own, while enabling you to use your instructional time effectively.

Begin with this simple model based on the pillars that support effective strategy instruction:

1. Introduce what you will be doing in a way that sets a purpose and motivates students' participation. (Have students buy into the lesson.)

2. Describe the strategy you want students to learn.

3. Model the strategy, providing verbal and visual reinforcements.

4. Apply the strategy while encouraging student interaction, furthering the scaffolding process.

5. Begin to release responsibility to students as you guide them toward independence: They do. You watch and assess.

6. Encourage students to generalize strategies so they gain the skills necessary to apply them across time and settings (sustain and maintain).

The following is an example of Tier 2 instruction with students who have yet to become thoughtful readers. They read through a passage without noticing when or why their comprehension breaks down. In order to encourage these students to self-monitor their comprehension and use their own words to summarize main ideas, I've utilized the strategy developed by Schumaker, Denton, and Deshler (1984) known as Read-Ask-Paraphrase, or RAP.

Introduce the Strategy: *OK, readers, I've noticed that when you are given a paragraph to read on your own, you look it over and quickly say you're done. So today, I'm going to show you a strategy that will help you slow down and really think about what you're reading.*

You have set the purpose for the lesson students are about to take part in, and you have helped them make a personal connection about why it is important for them to listen and learn.

Describe the Strategy: *You're going to learn about a strategy called RAP today. This strategy can be used anytime you read. RAP stands for Read, Ask questions, and Paraphrase. When we paraphrase, we use our own words to summarize what we just read. The RAP strategy will help you get a better idea about what you are reading. Here's how it works: You read one paragraph or section of a book and then stop. After you stop reading, you jot down questions that you have about what you are reading. Then you make sure that you can* *summarize the paragraph or section in your own words—which is the same thing as paraphrasing.*

Model the Strategy: *Why don't I show you what I'm talking about? Usually I read silently—but because I'm showing you how I use the RAP strategy, I'm going to read this paragraph from* Flying Solo, *by Ralph Fletcher, out loud so you can hear exactly what I'm thinking as I use this strategy, and then it will be your turn.* (After reading the first paragraph, section, or page, stop.) *Now, I'm going to stop reading and ask questions that come to my mind about the main idea. I'm wondering this: Why doesn't Rachel enjoy school? She seems to enjoy reading and learning—and she likes her teacher—so why doesn't she like school? I wonder if she is being teased by other kids. Now, I'll summarize, or paraphrase, what I've read: So far, this story is about a girl who likes her teacher, but she doesn't like school.*

Notice that I modeled the RAP strategy. As you model, it is a good idea to use a visual element, such as a poster or chart, to help guide students.

R—Read a paragraph

A—Ask yourself: *What was the main idea, and what were two details in this paragraph?*

P—Put the main idea and details into your own words.

Apply Interactively: Read the next section of the story. Continue to model your question asking and your paraphrasing. This time, encourage students to contribute their own questions and paraphrasing. If some students are not contributing, suggest that they agree or disagree with another peer's contribution to ensure that each student feels part of the learning process. You could also incorporate the Every-Student-Responds Strategies discussed on pages 35–38 to encourage students to participate within this interactive group time.

Apply Independently: When the time feels appropriate, have students read a section on their own and jot down their questions. Come together as a group and allow students to share their questions and paraphrasing about what they have read so far. As students are independently applying the RAP strategy, use this time to check in with those who were reluctant to share during the group activity. This will give you a better idea of who needs further support.

Generalizing: Emphasize to your students that the learning that took place today will be valuable during other reading experiences as well.

OK, today you worked hard to remember to slow down your reading by reading one paragraph at a time and then making sure that you understood what you just read before going on. I know that RAP can help you at other times during the day when you need to summarize main ideas in your own words. Be on the lookout for other times during the school day when you can use this strategy.

Make sure that you revisit this strategy by following up with what you noticed students doing over time. In addition, make sure that students are also able to notice and explain how this strategy has helped to deepen their comprehension.

Tier 2 instruction allows you to provide additional support to struggling students through explicit, small-group instruction. Sometimes this is all it takes for a student to master a particular content area, concept, or skill and then he or she is ready to move on to Tier 1 without any additional supports.

In order to tell whether students are responding positively to instruction, you must have assessment practices in place that guide your planning for effective instruction and positive learning outcomes for students. The next chapter offers an in-depth discussion of assessment options.

Chapter 3

Assessments to Guide Instruction and Intervention

Assessment is something we must think about before, during, and after each lesson. Sometimes assessment simply means monitoring students' understanding through observation, while it can also refer to more formal assessments like quizzes and tests. Whatever method of assessment you choose, it must be ongoing and meaningful. When planned and implemented effectively, assessment becomes the means to illuminate a dimly lit pathway. It helps us find our way as we strive to create optimal learning experiences for our students. And assessment is crucial in the RTI framework.

At the heart of the Tier 2 RTI process is the monitoring of students' progress. The data we gain from student performance informs all of our decisions regarding instruction and student placement within RTI. We use the data we collect to decide whether a student is responding to instruction. Overall, four types of assessment guide a comprehensive assessment plan within RTI:

- Universal screening for all students (Tier 1)
- Progress monitoring (Tier 2: weekly, biweekly, or monthly; Tier 3: more intensive—daily or weekly)
- Diagnostic (at-risk students at any tier)
- Outcome (all students at any tier)

Basic RTI Assessment Plan

Tier 3
Intensive Progress Monitoring
(*daily or weekly*)

Tier 2
Progress Monitoring
(*weekly, bi-weekly, or monthly*)

Tier 1
Universal Screening/Benchmark
(*all students*)

Universal Screening Assessments

Screening assessments are administered school-wide to all students as an initial baseline to identify those who may not be meeting, or who exceed, grade-level expectations. These assessments are reliable, valid, and quick measures of students' overall ability and the critical skills known to predict achievement. Students who are not meeting grade-level expectations are "red-flagged." For example, a student who struggles with reading comprehension because he has difficulty figuring out unfamiliar vocabulary words in context would be placed on a list of students who need closer assessment, to determine if he is truly struggling or if he just had a difficult time with testing that day. Screening assessment results can function as a starting point for instruction, or they may indicate a need for further evaluation.

Progress Monitoring Assessments

Teachers use progress monitoring assessments for students they have identified through the screening assessments and classroom performances as struggling with whole-class instruction. These students fall below the established benchmarks and are at risk for not reaching academic success within Tier 1 alone. The assessment process identifies areas in need of improvement, and students receive instruction that focuses on these specific needs. According to Mellard, Fuchs, and McKnight (2006), three to five students in any given class often require additional support. Let's take a look at an example.

James is a fourth grader in Ms. Laurine's class who demonstrates difficulty with reading. During the screening assessment, he shows weakness in the area of fluency, which affects his comprehension. Ms. Laurine has arranged for additional instructional supports during reading workshop time. She works with James and other students in a small group three times per week to strengthen their fluency while the rest of the class is involved in workshop activities. Each week, she briefly checks the progress of his fluency skills. In one of these checks, Ms. Laurine notices that James stops after reading each word. She also observes that he is able to read most of the high-frequency words with sufficient accuracy. Each progress check Ms. Laurine administers includes a quick miscue analysis. As James is reading aloud, she writes down the words that present difficulty. Using this method, she guides James to review his miscues.

After four to six weeks, Ms. Laurine feels it is time to make a decision: If James is making progress, she will continue with whole-class instruction, along with the additional small-group fluency instruction. If he is not making progress, she will decide whether to give him more time with the small group or to alter her instructional methods during Tier 1 and/or Tier 2 in some way. If instructional changes are necessary, Ms. Laurine will make adjustments either by allowing James more time to practice the strategies or by choosing another strategy, such as visualization techniques. In addition to guiding James's fluency and pacing, she will guide him to stop after a short section to discuss what he pictures in his mind while reading. She will then encourage James to draw a quick sketch to summarize the story so far. The goal of these visualizing exercises is for James to begin focusing on what is happening in the text, rather than on just reading the words.

Teachers periodically administer brief progress monitoring assessments (often as short as one minute in length) to Tier 2 and Tier 3 students to determine whether they are responding to instruction and making sufficient progress. They collect and evaluate this assessment data throughout the school year for the following purposes:

- To determine the rate of a student's progress
- To provide information on the effectiveness of instruction and to modify the intervention as needed
- To identify additional information that fosters student achievement
- To analyze and interpret gaps between benchmarks and student achievement

Progress monitoring answers the following questions: "Is this student responding to instruction and intervention? If not, why not?" "Is the lack of progress due to a lack of consistent high-quality instruction—or is a true disability holding the student back?" The data collected from the progress-monitoring assessments provides insight into whether the gap between grade-level expectations and a student's performance is closing, or at least being maintained. Perhaps a change is needed within the instructional approach, or perhaps the student just needs more time within the current instructional model.

Deciding on the next steps of the RTI process is not an exact science. The process begins with analyzing the student's performance data. If the student is making slow but steady progress, more instructional time might be needed. If the student's performance is regressing or staying the same, a new approach would probably be best. These decisions are not to be taken lightly. Collaboration with colleagues is necessary to guide this review process.

Diagnostic Assessments

Students identified as at-risk by the universal screening process receive a diagnostic reading assessment that measures their skills within the five components of reading:

- Vocabulary
- Phonemic awareness
- Phonics
- Fluency
- Comprehension

Administered several times throughout the school year, the diagnostic assessment helps teachers gear instruction toward the specific needs of their students by providing in-depth, reliable information as to why a student might be struggling. The data collected from these assessments provides the basis for planning targeted, effective instruction and interventions. Although diagnostic assessments may be time-consuming and are often expensive, they provide reliable data that can easily be used to plan powerful instruction. Here are some examples of diagnostic assessments.

Dynamic Indicator of Basic Early Literary Skills (DIBELS): The DIBELS assessments are a series of timed tests designed to determine fluency in the areas of letter naming, initial sound, phoneme segmentation, nonsense words, and oral reading.

Visit dibels.uoregon.edu/ to learn more. You can register for a free account and downloadable materials at dibels.uoregon.edu/measures.

Peabody Picture Vocabulary Test (PPVT): The PPVT measures expressive vocabulary and word retrieval in Standard American English. It requires students to identify the word called out by the tester by pointing to one of four pictures. This is an untimed test that takes about 15 minutes to administer and is appropriate for grades 2 through adult. For more information see psychcorp.pearsonassessments.com/HAIWEB/ Cultures/en-us/Productdetail.htm?Pid=PAa30700.

Accelerated Reading: After reading a chapter book, students through eighth grade can take a computer-based comprehension test made up of questions about the text. These questions assess knowledge of basic facts about the book and of the characters' motivations. For more information visit: www.renlearn.com/products.aspx.

Teacher-Created Assessments: Teachers often find that the most valuable assessment is one that they create themselves. This often takes the form of a checklist of reading indicators, such as the ability to explain vocabulary words, read fluently, express what was read, or identify the main idea. (See curriculum-based measurements and formative assessments on pages 50–59.)

Outcome Assessments

An outcome assessment is meant to assess exactly what its name indicates—the outcome of students' overall learning. Often used for school, district, or state reporting purposes, these summative assessments provide feedback about the overall effectiveness of instructional programs by measuring learning that has occurred during a period of time or over the school year. They include unit tests, midterms, final exams, and state tests.

The Purpose of Assessments

RTI's instruction and assessment cycles require that you make many decisions as you evaluate student performance. Some assessments are mandatory and are considered to be the primary mode in assessing students along the RTI cycle. These include the benchmark and outcome assessments that school districts have chosen, which are consistently implemented across classrooms. Students' performance on these assessments is compared to grade-level norms for their peers locally and nationally; for example, summative assessments may include district- and state-level tests. In addition to summative assessments, you are free to implement any supporting forms of assessment you feel would strengthen your instruction. These additional performance, or formative, assessments offer valuable information as you plan instruction. The main purpose of assessment is to define instruction and target specific goals to guide students to achieve. Consistent, reliable assessment procedures must be in place in order for students within Tier 2 instruction to meet with success.

Progress Monitoring: Powerful Tier 2 Assessment

Progress monitoring is a research-based strategy that measures student achievement through the use of targeted instruction and frequent (e.g., weekly, monthly) assessment of academic performance. Based on the information collected, you can chart a student's progress toward his or her individual goals and make adjustments when necessary—including adjustments to instructional approaches. Progress monitoring is an ongoing practice that allows teachers to pinpoint when a student is having difficulty and when a student is beginning to show progress. The Web site of the National Center on Student Progress Monitoring (studentprogress.org) offers valuable resources for progress monitoring.

Within the RTI framework, classroom teachers must monitor their students' progress systematically. They must be able to show evidence that Adam is struggling, and the evidence must indicate that they have implemented high-quality, research-based core instruction. The data must also show how Adam has responded to that instruction over time. Keep in mind that this systematic procedure needs to be in place only for students whom you deem not to have responded to Tier 1 instruction. As the diagram below shows, the flow of instruction and assessment within the Tier 2 process aligns naturally with a teacher's daily tasks.

Tier 2 Flow of Instruction and Assessment

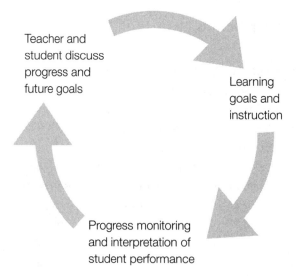

Teacher and student discuss progress and future goals

Learning goals and instruction

Progress monitoring and interpretation of student performance

Summing Up the Basics of Progress Monitoring

- Progress monitoring is a quick measure (as brief as one minute) that shows student progress on a targeted skill.

- Teachers use progress monitoring to guide their instructional decisions. It indicates whether what they are doing is effective and informs them if an instructional change is necessary.

- Progress monitoring evaluates the quality of instruction; typically, students who demonstrate progress can be said to be receiving high-quality instruction.

- Probes refer to questions that review and challenge students in order to encourage progress in the mastery of a skill.

- Teachers can create their own progress monitoring tools or they may use commercially developed probes. (See page 61 for a list.)

What the Research Says:

- High-level student monitoring enables teachers to become more reflective practitioners. When teachers and students have an active dialogue about specific strategies, skills, and personal performance, it encourages students to understand what actions they need to take in order to improve learning. Students are more aware of their learning and effort, and they achieve higher grades (Fuchs & Fuchs 2007).

- As part of progress monitoring, teachers can involve students in creating graphs to depict their progress in a quick visual format. Graphing can motivate students to strive to reach higher levels of learning by fostering a greater sense of responsibility for their own education (Davis, Fuchs, Fuchs, Whinnery 1995).

- Progress monitoring effectively informs instruction and guides teachers to make appropriate instructional changes (Fuchs & Fuchs 2007).

- Progress monitoring data is a strong predictor of students' achievement on standardized tests (Good, Simmons, & Kame'enui 2001).

Why Monitor Progress?

- To make certain that instructional interventions are working

- To provide objective documentation about student performance toward mastery of a specific skill level

- To provide information as you plan instruction

- To motivate students by showing them their present level of performance, engage them in the learning process, and inspire them to achieve at higher levels

Assessment strategies in progress monitoring can take many forms, including curriculum-based measurement and classroom assessments purchased by the district or created by teachers.

TEACHER-FRIENDLY PROGRESS MONITORING: THE BENEFITS OF CURRICULUM-BASED MEASUREMENT

Curriculum-Based Measurement (CBM) is a well-known, researched-based monitoring tool that Stan Deno and Phyllis Mirkin developed in the late 1970s. CBM serves three key functions:

- It indicates whether the student is learning.
- It indicates the rate at which the student is learning.
- It offers classroom teachers a simple, easy-to-use tool to inform instruction.

CBM scores may be used to monitor students' weekly or monthly progress as they gain competence toward reaching grade-level expectations.

Another tool for monitoring progress is AIMSweb, which provides teachers with the norms to evaluate their students against their peers nationwide. Some districts use this resource to organize their assessment procedures. For more information, visit www. aimsweb.com.

Teacher-Friendly, Curriculum-Based Measurements for Tier 2 Reading Instruction: Word Identification Fluency

In this CBM, a student reads from a list of high-frequency or grade-level words in order to demonstrate his or her reading fluency. After the student reads these words aloud for one minute, the teacher records the number of words the student read correctly.

Passage reading fluency: The student reads a passage aloud for one minute. The score is the number of words read correctly.

Maze fluency: In this comprehension assessment, students read a passage between 150 and 400 words. The first sentence of the passage is left intact, but in the following sentences, every seventh word has been deleted and replaced with three possible choices in parentheses. One is the word that appears in the passage; the other two are distracters that test the reader's comprehension skills. The student selects the best choice while reading the passage. The score is the number of correct word choices. The example on the next page shows the first three sentences of an assessment using "Spaghetti" in *Every Living Thing* by Cynthia Rylant.

It was evening, and people sat outside, talking quietly among themselves. On the stoop of a tall (*building, request, fail*) of crumbling bricks and rotting wood (*think, recklessly, sat*) a boy. His name was Gabriel (*appear, and, raspy*) he wished for some company.

CREATING YOUR OWN PROGRESS MONITORING ASSESSMENTS

Assessment is all about gauging the learning of our students. Meaningful assessment answers the question, "Did the students master the skill I aimed to teach them?" Curriculum-Based Assessments provide a simple way to answer this question. They can also provide evidence of student performance, and you can use these results to make informed instructional decisions. Curriculum-Based Assessments are an effective way to organize important assessment practices. Here's how they work, in six easy steps.

1. **Decide the skill that you will be measuring, based on a student's area of need.**

   - Write down a specific learning goal based on the student's need as determined by screening assessments, classroom assessments, and performance; for example, *Brittany will use context clues to define up to five new vocabulary words as she reads four of the five reading passages.*

   - Typical reading skills to address when creating learning goals include word-list reading for accuracy, fluency rate, vocabulary, listening, and critical-thinking comprehension skills.

2. **Create or locate quick assessments.** These assessment probes provide a glance at how the student is performing on a targeted skill.

   - Once you select a reading skill, create a one-minute assessment tool. This tool can be a list of specific words to assess for word accuracy, a short passage to assess fluency, or a short passage with five comprehension questions.

   - Locate assessment probes by doing an Internet search or visiting the Web sites on page 62.

3. **Identify a baseline.**

   - In order to find a student's baseline, assess him or her on three separate days over the course of one week and then average the scores.

4. **Map out a timeline for achieving specific learning goals.** (Review your learning goal from step 1.) Look at the student's baseline and determine the length of the assessment period. You will need to monitor progress either weekly or biweekly for four to six weeks, but an eight- or 12-week time frame might also be effective, depending on the student.

    ■ Tier 2 intervention should be monitored once per week, biweekly, or monthly, depending on the student.

    ■ Learning expectations and goals should meet with the learner's current abilities, while challenging the student to catch up to his or her peers.

    ■ Compare the student's performance to an established norm or a sample of exemplary student work that shows proficiency in the skill you are assessing.

    ■ Create manageable learning expectations for your student.

5. **Create a graph.**

    ■ Create a line graph by labeling the x-axis with the date and the y-axis with the student's percentage of accuracy in the skill.

    ■ Plot the baseline and determine the goal point to coincide with your instructional time frame. Connect the two plots in order to visually depict the target line for your instruction over the next few weeks.

6. **Enter the student's progress while continually comparing it to the target line.**

    ■ Over the weeks of assessment checkpoints, evaluate whether the student is progressing toward the established goal.

    ■ After three assessment checkpoints, notice how close the student is to the target line. If after four to six weeks he or she is not close to reaching the target line, think about implementing another research-based strategy in your instruction.

This graph serves as effective documentation as you communicate your student's performance to colleagues at your RTI team meeting and to parents. It is also an ideal motivator for your students, who enjoy plotting their progress as well as monitoring their skills and performance.

The goal of Curriculum-Based Measures is to help you plan activities that quickly produce student work samples that show evidence of how he or she is learning. Creating these quick measures can become second nature as you strive to understand how your teaching decisions relate to your students' learning. Systematic analysis of student work, such as the one shown in the diagram on the next page, supplies the information you need to plan for instruction and provides guidelines for reflecting on student work.

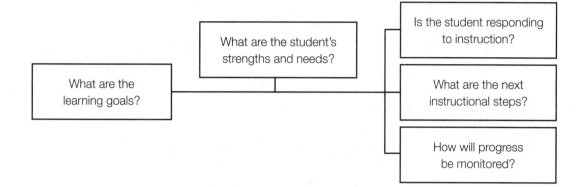

This series of reflective prompts can help guide you in taking a closer look at evidence of a student's performance. The first two questions begin the process by zooming in on the specific purpose of the evidence. Once you have identified the learning objective, you can look to see how close the student came to achieving that goal. The natural next step is to identify the student's strengths and needs in relation to the learning goal and the skill(s) needed to achieve that goal. The answer to the next question, "Is the student responding to instruction?" is a critical point in the reflective process. It guides us naturally as we consider what the next instructional steps are, and it also helps us decide if the current assessment methods are effective. If the student is responding to instruction, then perhaps he or she just needs more time and practice. If the student is not responding, then you may need to make instructional changes, such as the following:

- Increase the amount of instructional time per week
- Modify or adapt your instructional strategies
- Implement a new instructional method

It is also ideal to collaborate with colleagues and to have a few like-minded teachers work with you to reflect on your students' work. In fact, setting up weekly group time for this purpose is a valuable way to strengthen your skills in using formative assessments.

Formative Assessment: The Key to Progress Monitoring

Formative assessments are a natural link to effective progress monitoring. The sole purpose of formative assessment is to inform instruction, not to assign a grade. This ongoing assessment process documents students' strengths and needs—perfect for all students—but it is especially valuable as you document progress for students who receive Tier 2 instruction. Cowie and Bell (1999) define formative assessments as "a bidirectional process between teacher and student to strengthen the connection between instruction and student's response to learning."

Discussed below are formative assessment procedures that you can implement within whole-class or small-group instruction.

GET UP AND GO (FOUR CORNERS)

This is a quick assessment tool that lets you assess what students know in a setting in which they are engaged and motivated to participate. The strategy is easy to prepare and simple to adapt for any grade level or topic. It involves the following steps:

- Label each corner of the room with a sign reading "Agree," "Disagree," "Strongly Agree," or "Strongly Disagree." You can also use the following signs: "Agreer," "Naysayer," "Questioner," "Elaborater." In any case, make the signs appropriate for the activity you are planning. If you want students to express and evaluate the degree of their agreement or disagreement, use the first set of signs above. If you would like students to simply agree or disagree and then explain their reasoning, then use the second set of signs.

- Read statements that support a topic you are teaching, and then have students express their thoughts by moving to the appropriate corner of the room.

- Give students within each group time to share their thinking. Walk around the room and listen in while taking anecdotal notes about which students can validate their thinking and which students need additional support.

RESPONSE NOTES

This quick activity shows students' thinking and comprehension levels during and after reading a text. It also provides an opportunity for students to reflect on their learning. Students are free to apply active reading strategies, such as the ones listed below. The idea is to encourage students to think more deeply as they organize their thinking. You will need to guide students to meaningfully respond. (See Chapter 6 on reading comprehension for ways of getting students to respond appropriately to text.) The types of strategies you decide to focus on will depend on the genre; but some types of thinking connect to all genres:

- Making predictions
- Asking questions

- Noticing interesting or new vocabulary words
- Summarizing key points and evaluating how the reader's ideas connect to the important ideas in the text

One of my colleagues, fourth-grade teacher Mary Conners, worked with me in an inclusion setting. We wrapped our instruction around modeling and guiding students to actively read and respond to what they read. We prepared a template to guide students' use of the strategies we hoped they would use before, during, and after reading. Mary printed this template on labels and gave one to each student to place in his or her response notebook as a checklist to guide thinking. After writing a response to the reading, students color coded each type of thinking in their response notebooks. For example, one student decided to highlight predicting in pink and questioning in blue. This student read through her responses and highlighted all of the sentences with evidence of her predictions in pink, all of her questions in blue, and so on. This color coding helped the student become aware of her thinking about what she read, which guided her toward more independent and frequent use of active reading strategies.

QUICK CHECKS

Quick Checks are brief assessments that differ from typical quizzes in that students receive immediate, specific feedback directly following the quiz. Both student and teacher learn at the moment of assessment how the student is performing and can discuss his or her strengths and needs for future learning. In a Quick Check, the student responds to multiple-choice or short-answer questions. There are two ways to provide feedback. One way is to have students take the quiz in pencil and have them grade themselves as you review the answers. Another way is to have students fold their paper vertically and then write their answers on the left side of the paper. Following the quiz, they copy their answers on the right side, then tear the paper in half and hand in the left side to you. The advantage here is that the students don't have the opportunity to change their answers. A group discussion can follow, in which a few students justify their correct responses and discuss any confusion or newfound knowledge resulting from their corrected responses.

Casey May 5	Casey May 5
1. B	1. B
2. A	2. A
3. A	3. A
4. C	4. C
5. D	5. D
6. A	6. A
7. C	7. C
8. B	8. B
9. A	9. A
10. C	10. C

INDIVIDUAL WHITEBOARDS

This tried-and-true strategy keeps your students engaged, and it doubles as an effective assessment tool. You can use individual whiteboards to assess vocabulary knowledge as well as comprehension, and these tools are easily incorporated into any part of a reading lesson. Simply prepare questions that require mastery of a particular skill. For example, if your targeted goal is to have students understand five vocabulary words, you can assess this goal by pausing at appropriate parts of the lesson and having students jot down their understanding of particular words or usage on their whiteboards. Students then hold their whiteboards overhead, and you get an immediate, clear picture of which students are applying and extending their knowledge and those who will need further instruction. This procedure works just as well with basic comprehension questions and deeper inferential questions. Students are actively involved and are accountable for completing the work. As the given topic unfolds and you facilitate the group discussion, student whiteboard responses provide immediate feedback to both you and them. And again, you can easily see who needs additional support.

MISCUE ANALYSIS

All readers use a cueing system to guide them to read words accurately. As readers become more experienced, this cueing system becomes a natural part of the reading process that they use with ease to figure out unknown words. Struggling readers often make miscues, or incorrect guesses. They read words or phrases inaccurately. As a result, comprehension breaks down and they cannot construct meaning from text. Miscue analysis is a tool for looking closely at the types of reading strategies a reader uses. Listening to the kinds of miscues a student makes when reading from a text will give you clues about how familiar the reader is with the content matter and how easy or difficult the text is to read. Reading tests cannot give this sort of information because reading is so much more than just looking closely at each letter and every word. Goodman (1969), who first coined the term "miscue analysis," based his approach on three "cueing" systems he believed to be at the foundation of the reading process.

Graphophonic: This visual cue allows the reader to use his or her knowledge of the relationship of letters to sounds and ask: *Does the word that I read look like the word on the page?*

Syntactic: The reader's knowledge of the way language works and the use of syntax, structure, and parts of speech guide him or her to ask: *Does this sound right?*

Semantic: The reader uses context clues and text features such as graphics to make meaning while reading. To support comprehension, the reader asks: *Does this make sense?*

Goodman was eager to disprove the idea that miscues were bad. He believed that the pattern of miscues could suggest a reader's strengths as well as his or her weaknesses. If we put together the miscues with what the learner can tell us about how those miscues were made, then we can begin to understand what is really going on when he or she reads a text.

The cueing systems that Goodman developed are useful in the following ways:

- As a window for the teacher to see what a student is thinking as he or she reads

- As a means to guide instruction aimed at strengthening specific skills

- As a means for observing reading behaviors during the administration of running records

Administering a Miscue Analysis

Preparation is the key to carrying out a meaningful miscue analysis. To be successful, you will need to create a distraction-free environment. You will also need to do the following:

- Select a reading passage that is appropriate for the reader based on his or her grade or performance level.

- Make two copies of the passage, one for the student and one for yourself.

- Put your copy on a clipboard so the student does not see you marking it up and making notes as he or she reads.

- Tell the student: *I want you to read aloud for one minute. Try to read each word. If you wait too long to read a word, I will tell you the word.* (Give the student three seconds to decode the word before you identify it.) *You may say "skip" if you feel you do not know the word. After one minute, I will tell you to stop.*

- A tape recorder with a microphone is useful if you want to listen to the student's reading again.

- As the student reads the passage, be ready to circle his or her miscues.

- Following the reading, record the miscues in a chart like the one shown on the next page. Write each word that the student skipped or misread and then put a check in the column of the cueing system. The chart will help you to notice the student's strengths and weaknesses. Analyzing the miscues will inform your instructional decisions about how to guide the student toward reading success.

The sample chart on the next page shows the performance of Kendra, a fourth grader, reading a passage from Anne Mazer's *The Amazing Days of Abby Hayes: Out of Sight, Out of Mind.* Here is what the teacher's notes looked like following Kendra's one-minute reading:

Text Word/ Word Read	Visual (Graphophonic)	Meaning (Semantic)	Structure (Syntactic)	Self-Corrected
quick/quiet	●	●		
laptop/little			●	
smirked/smelled	●	●		
leave/live	●	●		yes
charge/change	●	●		

Kendra read the following sentences:

1. "Isabel tapped a quick sentence onto the screen." (Kendra substituted *quiet* for *quick*.)

2. "She was taking notes on a laptop computer." (Kendra read *laptop* as *little*.)

3. "She smirked at her twin and slammed the door shut." (Kendra read *smirked* as *smelled*.)

4. "Did Mom and Dad leave you in charge?" (Kendra had two miscues in this sentence: She read *leave* as *live* and *charge* as *change*.)

In this sample, Kendra consistently used the graphophonic and syntactic cues as she read. As her miscues indicate, she is clearly not reading for meaning. Her single instance of self-correction indicates that she is not stopping to notice that the words she is reading are not making sense. The teacher now knows to guide Kendra to continue using her strengths, but to pause more often to ask herself, "Does this make sense? What could this word be so that the sentence makes sense?"

You can also use a chart like the one shown below to keep track of the types of cues the student uses to guide his or her understanding of the text.

Analysis of Errors Chart

	Seldom	Sometimes	Usually
Uses Visual Cues (graphophonic)			
Uses Structure Cues (syntactic)			
Uses Meaning Cues (semantic)			

Retrospective Miscue Analysis

As students get older, they grow increasingly capable of taking on more responsibility for their learning. By providing opportunities for students to gain insight into their own thinking process before, during, and after reading (Goodman & Marek 1996), retrospective miscue analysis is an effective means of guiding them to become more independent, reflective readers. In classrooms where teachers use running records and miscue analysis to monitor progress, students can easily become a part of the process of determining their own areas of strength and need. Here are some questions you can ask students to help them reflect on their reading:

- *What was your miscue?*
- *Did you self-correct?*
- *Why do you think you made this miscue?*
- *How did the miscue affect your understanding of the text?*
- *What do readers need to do in order to understand what they read?*
- *What does this make you think about as you are reading?*

Portfolio Assessments

In "Student Portfolios: Classroom Uses," a 1993 consumer guide issued by the U.S. Department of Education, research showed that students at all grade levels viewed assessment as something done to their work by someone else. Students showed very little understanding of what evaluating their own work entailed beyond the "percentage right" or the letter grade issued by a teacher. Portfolios can serve as a tool for guiding students to strengthen their critical thinking skills as they evaluate their own work and reflect on their progress. Additionally, students can notice their personal growth, which can contribute toward positive views of themselves as learners. In "Portfolio Research: A Slim Collection," Herman and Winters (1994) note the following:

> *Well-designed portfolios represent important, contextualized learning that requires complex thinking and expressive skills. Traditional tests have been criticized as being insensitive to local curriculum and instruction, and assessing not only student achievement but aptitude. Portfolios are being heralded as vehicles that provide a more equitable and sensitive portrait of what students know and are able to do. Portfolios encourage teachers and schools to focus on important student outcomes, provide parents and the community with credible evidence of student achievement, and inform policy and practice at every level of the educational system.*

Generally, a portfolio is a systematic collection of a variety of examples of student performance. These can range from a teacher's anecdotal notes to student work samples collected over time that depict developmental and academic progress. Careful consideration must be given to what goes into a portfolio. If the selection process is not given the proper attention and consideration, the portfolio may end up being merely a file of random student work (Valencia 1990). Here are the key points to keep in mind for portfolio assessment:

- Systematically gathers evidence to show progress over time
- Transfers responsibility of learning to the student
- Promotes improved self-image or self-esteem and a sense of ownership
- Provides a means for weaving instruction and assessment together
- Allows for real-world experiences

- Provides a relief from test anxiety

- Allows for multiple assessments within a child-centered classroom

- Leaves room for individualizing

- Is a valuable resource that provides effective communication between school and parents

HOW TO SET UP PORTFOLIO ASSESSMENTS

The purpose of keeping a portfolio as an assessment tool within the RTI framework is to assess a student's progress over time. Keeping this purpose in mind will help you decide what to include in the portfolio. Here are a few suggestions:

- Early and later pieces of work

- Early and later quizzes and tests with scores

- First drafts and final drafts of responses to reading

- Student's written goals and reflections related to reading

Set up conference time to meet one-to-one with students to review their progress and to guide them to reflect on their accomplishments and future goals.

Progress monitoring is the pulse that keeps the RTI process moving smoothly and effectively. When you take the time to develop consistent, ongoing techniques, students learn to take responsibility for their learning and understand what they need to do to remain active in the learning process. And you get to keenly apply what you learn about a student's strengths and needs to make the best instructional decisions for that student.

Progress Monitoring Web Sites

The following Web sites offer a wide variety of research-validated resources about monitoring your students' reading progress:

- The National Center on Student Progress Monitoring shares a variety of commercially available tools: www.studentprogress.org.

- DIBELS: https://dibels.uoregon.edu

- AIMSweb: www.aimsweb.com

- Jim Wright, a New York psychologist, created Intervention Central as a resource for various interventions and progress monitoring tools.
  - ➡ www.interventioncentral.org/index.php/cbm-warehouse
  - ➡ www.interventioncentral.org/index.php/tools/193-cbm-maze-passage-generator

- Curriculum-Based Measurement support for K–12:
  - ➡ www.cbmnow.com
  - ➡ www.easycbm.com

Chapter 4

Vocabulary

Vocabulary development is one key to developing critical literacy skills. Research tells us that most vocabulary is learned indirectly. Children begin to add to their repertoire of vocabulary by listening to stories read to them by adults, listening and speaking in conversations with adults, and later through conversations with peers, as well as by reading extensively on their own (Pence & Justice 2008). Research also tells us that some vocabulary must be taught directly, through word-learning strategies, repetition and review, along with direct instruction. All students need high-quality vocabulary instruction along with consistent exposure to vocabulary through conversations and reading a variety of texts. Some students, however, require additional time to interact with language in order to extend their vocabulary acquisition. It is this kind of Tier 2 strategic instruction that is the focus of this chapter.

Vocabulary and the Common Core State Standards

The CCSS weave vocabulary and conventions through all reading, writing, listening, and speaking experiences. Therefore, vocabulary should not be taught in isolation, but rather, it should be integrated within all content and skills as we guide students to develop into independent, effective learners and communicators.

Vocabulary and Reading Comprehension

Vocabulary knowledge is the foundation of reading comprehension. It is not enough to simply decode words; true reading only occurs when students understand the words they read. Enthusiastic readers tend to have broad vocabularies because of their frequent exposure to words in print. Struggling readers tend to read less, so they often have very limited vocabularies. As a result, their reading comprehension skills suffer. High-quality Tier 1 instruction often helps these struggling readers find success, but sometimes additional instructional strategies are needed. To comprehend academic texts, students require a higher level of skills, including an understanding of academic language and the use of comprehension strategies.

When Students Struggle With Vocabulary

Successful readers set a purpose for reading and draw on prior knowledge, experiences, and a variety of strategies to make meaning from text. Successful readers are strategic readers; they continually monitor their comprehension and, as needed, will stop and revisit their "tool kit" of reading strategies to gain a better understanding of what they are reading. Proficient readers often find themselves questioning or reorganizing text, summarizing, analyzing, and making connections to other subjects and contexts (NICHD, 2007).

Struggling readers, by contrast, find expository text challenging because they rely on too few or ineffective strategies, do not monitor their understanding, and/or cannot transfer the strategies they use in casual reading to academic texts. When reading is frustrating or laborious, students are not motivated to read. They turn their energy to conjuring up ways to avoid reading and often have difficulty learning in many subject areas. We cannot control the knowledge and experiences that students bring to the classroom; however, we can help students access or retrieve knowledge about a particular subject to help them make connections to the new knowledge we introduce. We cannot wave a magic wand and double students' vocabulary overnight, but we can provide them with tools to unlock the meaning of unfamiliar words. We can offer opportunities for students to use new words in meaningful contexts. We cannot force comprehension to take place, but we can guide our students to monitor their own understanding of texts. To accomplish the task of helping students become proficient readers and learners, we need to have an assortment of useful strategies to assist struggling readers and build their vocabulary, fluency, and comprehension.

Vocabulary and Tier 2 Instruction

Students who struggle with some aspect of reading typically begin to express their opinions about reading and their views of themselves as readers as they reach the intermediate grades. Far too often, we hear students say things like, "I don't like reading" or "I can't read this, it's too hard." These are indications that something more might be going on. We must be diligent in identifying why students are expressing negative views about themselves as readers. Turning around the attitudes of these students may simply depend on exposing them to effective problem-solving strategies that they can use when comprehension breaks down.

Students with a limited vocabulary often demonstrate this weakness through a lack of fluency when speaking. You might notice that these students pause often without expressing their ideas clearly. For example, when discussing the vocabulary word *evaluate*, a student might say something like, "Oh, yeah, I know what it means to evaluate. It's when you . . . um . . . say something about . . . um . . . you know. . . ." This kind of incoherent verbal expression is often an indication of poor word-retrieval skills.

Students often have trouble summarizing the important points of a nonfiction text because they are unable to identify the key words that express the text's main ideas. Some students are able to learn new vocabulary words but cannot explain what these words mean or apply the meaning to their own experiences or prior knowledge.

Students often struggle with vocabulary for the following reasons:

- They lack enthusiasm for learning about words.
- They have poor memory skills, so they struggle with retention.
- They have had limited exposure to enriching vocabulary at home and/or at school.
- They have difficulty applying word-learning strategies.

When students' vocabulary fails to grow, educators and parents must take notice and begin to look for the causes. Is the student struggling because of a learning and language disability? Is the difficulty due to a lack of effective instruction? This is where RTI enters the picture: It will help us determine the reasons for a student's performance. For example, when struggling students respond positively to whole-class instruction, it is evident that their difficulties were due to a previous lack of instruction. The solution in this case is continued high-quality core instruction with the whole class. If students continue to struggle at the Tier 1 level, they continue to receive whole-class instruction with added small-group strategic instruction at the Tier 2 level.

Effective strategic instruction can connect students' current level of performance with specific strategies that strengthen the vocabulary skills they need to succeed. Use the chart below to help you match your students' needs with the vocabulary strategies discussed in this chapter.

If students' performance reveals ...	Then try ...	To ...
rote memorization of vocabulary words and difficulty remembering meaning of words	Marzano's Six Steps, pp. 68–70	create opportunities for students to attach personal connections and a deeper understanding to academic vocabulary.
difficulty identifying important words and determining their importance	Vocabulary Self-Collection, pp. 84–85	guide students to construct meaning from text and remember the meaning of academic vocabulary.
a lack of background knowledge about an upcoming unit of study	Marzano's Six Steps, pp. 68–70 List-Group-Label, pp. 71–72 Predict-O-Gram, pp. 86–87	create opportunities for students to connect, paraphrase, and transfer an understanding of words to future reading, speaking, and listening experiences.
difficulty paraphrasing vocabulary words and concepts	Synonym Links, pp. 73–74 Anything Goes, p. 82	encourage students to identify academic vocabulary and explain the meaning of key ideas in their own words.
difficulty with word retrieval and applying vocabulary in writing assignments	Synonym Links, pp. 73–74 Anything Goes, p. 82	strengthen students' ability to apply what they know about the meaning of specific vocabulary through written expression.

If students' performance reveals . . .	Then try . . .	To . . .
difficulty with word retrieval and applying vocabulary while listening and speaking	Lansdown Word Cards, pp. 78–80 Word Storm, pp. 83–84	increase students' ability to apply their understanding of words while listening and speaking.
difficulty connecting previously taught vocabulary to new learning	Frayer Model, pp. 75–77 Word Storm, pp. 83–84	create opportunities for students to connect, remember, generalize, and understand what words mean.
difficulty figuring out unknown words	Synonym Links, pp. 73–74 Lansdown Word Cards, pp. 78–80 Catch That Word, pp. 80–81	encourage students to use the context to gain meaning and transfer understanding of words and concepts across a variety of texts and subject areas.

Marzano's Six Steps

When to Use: *Before, During, and After Reading*

Purpose: *To engage students in the process of learning and truly understanding words.*

Robert Marzano and Debra J. Pickering (2005) offer a vocabulary notebook template that guides students toward attaining a deeper level of vocabulary knowledge. They state, "When students copy the teacher's explanation or description of a term instead of generating their own explanation, the results are not as strong. Ideally, student explanations should come from their own lives."

The notebook provides a place where students can begin to express their understanding by writing a term in their own words, providing an additional example, creating an illustration, and evaluating their own understanding of the word on a scale of 1–4. Let's take a look at how the six-step process could play out in a typical Tier 2 small group.

Process: Follow these steps:

1. Give students a description, an explanation, or an example of the new term. For example, as students preview a text on colonial times, identify the word *colony*. This word is central to understanding how the 13 colonies became the United States, and it comes up frequently in the ongoing social studies curriculum. Here's how step 1 might sound:

    Teacher: *As we begin to study the 13 colonies, it is important to understand what a colony is. When a country or a region is under the political control of a distant country, we say that it is a colony of another country. Now see how we can use this definition to help us understand more about the 13 colonies. Let's reread this section of the text and look at the map to help us understand this part of our United States history.*

2. Ask students to paraphrase your description, explanation, or example.

    Teacher: *Let's take some time to put this definition of a colony together with what you have been reading. How does the definition connect to what you already know and to what you are learning?*

    Maya: *We just read about how England wanted to gain power and wealth. So colonists came to North America to look for them.*

Teacher: *That's right, so how does our understanding of a colony help us understand what was going on at that time?*

Tyler: *Well, people from England came to North America and decided to settle here, but England still tried to control them.*

Maya: *So that's it: People who settled in the 13 colonies were not originally from North America, and they were controlled by their original country of England.*

3. Have students construct a pictorial or symbolic representation of the term. In a lesson on the 13 colonies, students might sketch a map of the colonies; some might make a sketch to indicate that the American colonies were controlled by a distant country. Others might simply jot down the words *North America* with an arrow pointing to the word *England*. This would remind them that the English settlers were living in North America, but they were still controlled by their distant, native country. Sketches should be quick representations that increase students' understanding and memory.

4. Engage students in activities that add to their knowledge.
   This is a good time for students to add terms to their vocabulary notebooks, using their own words while adding examples, making connections, and creating a sketch or symbol to deepen their understanding or help them remember the meaning. In addition, students can evaluate their own level of understanding of the word.

5. Periodically ask students to discuss the terms with one another.
   Stop the discussion intermittently to ask students if they can add their thinking to someone else's. If you notice someone is still struggling to put the terms in his or her own words, you could have that student repeat what another student has said in order to maintain engagement and aid comprehension. Encourage students to enter the key points of the discussion in their notebooks.

6. Involve students in games that involve playing with the terms.
   Be sure to find time for your students to play games that deepen their understanding of key vocabulary words. *Vocabulary Games for the Classroom,* by Robert J. Marzano and Lindsay Carleton, is full of games that ask students to apply their understanding of vocabulary words as they connect the words to a specific topic. More hands-on ideas that you can apply to your next vocabulary lesson can be found here: http://jc-schools.net/tutorials/vocab/strategies.html.

   Marzano's research has demonstrated the effectiveness of these six steps at every grade level from kindergarten through high school. Apply the first three steps when you introduce a new word to students. A few days later, review the new term using steps 4–6, which don't have to be implemented in any particular sequence. Note, however, this strategy works more effectively if all of them are used. Marzano's research has given us the tools we have always wanted to make vocabulary meaningful, engaging, and anything but dull, rote, dictionary work.

For more about academic vocabulary instruction, I highly suggest *Building Academic Vocabulary*, by Robert Marzano and Debra Pickering. In addition, numerous activities, games, and word lists are available online. Visit Marzano's own Web site to learn more about how to connect his research to your instruction: www.marzanoresearch.com/products/catalog.aspx?group=6.

Use the Strategy:

- To activate students' background knowledge of word meanings
- To preview targeted vocabulary words before reading to strengthen comprehension
- To review vocabulary following a reading
- To build students' long-term memory of key terms across content areas

Tier 2 Formative Assessments

✓ Take anecdotal notes as students participate in group discussions:
During and after instruction, jot down what you noticed with regard to each student's participation, attention, and application of skills. Also note whether reteaching is needed and which academic goal to include in the next small-group meeting. Anecdotal notes can serve as a valuable tool to help you discern how well a student is responding to specific strategies, and may be a key indicator for future instructional decisions.

✓ Read students' vocabulary notebooks:
Students' written expression will be a good indicator of their level of understanding. In addition to their oral expression during class discussion, you will be able to see whether they are able to apply specific concepts independently.

List-Group-Label

When to Use: *Before and After Reading*

Purpose: *To activate background knowledge and increase vocabulary.*

Developed from the work of Hilda Taba (1967), List-Group-Label helps students activate background knowledge about a topic and increase their knowledge of words and academic vocabulary while applying categorization and organization skills (Blachowicz & Fisher 2002).

Materials:

» chart paper and marker

» index cards

» reproducible: Anecdotal Notes, page 129

» reproducible: List-Group-Label, page 130

Process: Follow these steps:

1. Begin by brainstorming a list of words and phrases that are associated with a topic. Ask students to collaborate to generate as many words as they can think of. List students' responses on the board or on chart paper. Here's how a lesson on communities might look:

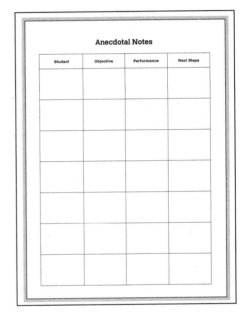

Teacher: *OK, readers, we've been learning a lot about communities. So, before we begin reading today, let's brainstorm a list of words we already know that connect to what we know about what makes a community.*

2. Read through the list to model correct pronunciation and spelling.

3. Next, work with students to sort words and phrases into groups. Encourage students to

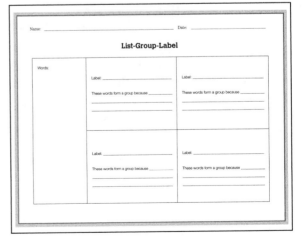

create a label for each group by thinking of a description or word that connects all the words within a group.

Teacher: *OK, let's begin to put these words into groups. We will have to decide which words are similar to each other. For example, we could start a group by putting "extended family" and "nuclear family" together because they both describe families. Or we could put "agriculture" and "irrigation" together because they both have to do with farming. You decide which groups you want to create by thinking about the reasons why you are putting the words in specific groups.*

4. Facilitate a discussion by asking students to explain the relationship between the words and phrases as they connect the vocabulary to the labels and topic. Have your small group of students talk in pairs before discussing with everyone at once. This will give all students a chance to engage in the discussion.

Use the Strategy:

- To introduce vocabulary
- To activate students' background knowledge and clarify their understanding
- To review terms prior to a test or before moving to the next unit of study

Tier 2 Formative Assessments

✓ Have students write words on index cards and place the word cards into groups. You can document each student's performance on an Anecdotal Notes reproducible. *Note*: You can use this reproducible with all the lessons in this book.

✓ Give a List-Group-Label graphic organizer to each student to complete. Studying students' completed graphic organizers of groups and labels will give you a window into their understanding and level of thinking. In addition, you will be able to identify any students who were unable to create groups in a way that makes sense, or those who were unable to create labels for their groups. Students' work samples will inform your decisions to continue reteaching concepts or moving on to new terms.

Synonym Links

When to Use: *Before, During, and After Reading*

Purpose: *To help students make connections to unfamiliar words.*

When students create synonyms, they expand their vocabulary and deepen their understanding of word meanings (Blachowicz & Fisher 2002). They also become more fluent in applying their understanding of vocabulary words. In addition, students practice the skill of evaluating words as they make decisions about which words connect as a synonym to the original word.

Materials:

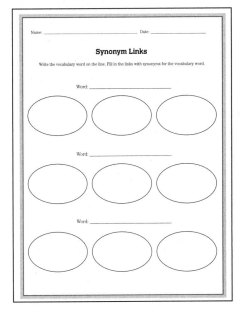

> » chart paper for teacher modeling and guided practice

> » reproducible: Synonym Links, page 131
>   (1 copy for each student)

> » marker

> » thesaurus

Process: Follow these steps:

1. Prepare a list of vocabulary words from a selected reading in advance or generate a list of words with students as they read. Base your vocabulary list on words that you identify as important for students to know for this particular text and subject area or words from the reading that you think students will encounter in a variety of texts and subject areas over time.

2. Facilitate a discussion to allow students to apply their background knowledge to generate three to five synonyms for each word. Students may use a thesaurus. Here's how this step might play out in a classroom:

   Teacher: *Today I'm going to show you how you can take one word and think of other words that mean the same thing. A word that means the same, or almost the same, as another word is called a synonym. Synonyms help us understand more words when we read. Watch me do this with the word "analyze." Remember, we used the word "analyze" when we were looking at the illustration of a colonial schoolhouse in our social studies text.*

At the beginning of our first link here, I'm going to write our word: "analyze." Now I'm going to think about what I remember about what this word means. When we were looking at the diagram of a schoolhouse during colonial times, we said we would analyze the diagram. And then we looked at each section of the picture. We broke the large picture into four sections to make sure we examined all of the details. So I'm going to say that a synonym for "analyze" could be "examine"—because we really did examine all of the details of that document.

Invite students to share their ideas. Finally, take out the thesaurus to check that the words students have chosen are actually synonyms, and then add any other synonyms to complete the Synonym Links graphic organizer. Have students complete the next word with you as you guide them to think it through. Provide this scaffolding until you notice that students need less input from you. At that point, allow them to fill in the synonym links independently. Remind them to use the thesaurus to check their words.

3. Guide students to use the Synonym Links reproducible for other words, as well as for recording new words in their vocabulary notebooks. Encourage them to notice words as they listen to others and also to include the synonyms in their writing and speaking. The goal is for students to independently make connections between words while expanding their vocabulary.

Use the Strategy:

- To enrich vocabulary and enhance comprehension of texts across genres and subjects

- To review words that students will encounter in a variety of texts

- To help students apply their understanding of words as they increase their awareness of how words relate to one another.

Tier 2 Formative Assessments

✓ Jot down anecdotal notes regarding students' participation in group discussion and completion of individual work. Pay attention to the accuracy and ease with which a student is able to create synonyms for given words. Students who choose accurate synonyms to depict the original word demonstrate a clear understanding of word meanings.

✓ Students' completed Synonym Links graphic organizer will provide evidence of how well their vocabulary and word knowledge is expanding.

Frayer Model

When to Use: *Before and After Reading*

Purpose: *To deepen students' level of understanding when learning unfamiliar vocabulary words.*

The Frayer Model provides a visual representation of a word to guide long-term learning. Research by Frayer, Frederick, and Klausmier at the University of Wisconsin suggests that students gain a stronger understanding of concepts when they develop a relationship between a word and its meaning. Frayer and her colleagues created a tool, the Frayer Model, to help students build an understanding of words during the process of reading (Frayer, Frederick, & Klausmier 1969). Using this model, students must first analyze a word through its definition and characteristics. They then provide examples and connect the word to their own experiences. By describing an example, students show that they can apply the meaning of the word. The Frayer Model guides students in truly understanding word meanings and concepts for long-term use, rather than just short-term memorization. Constructing the meaning of a word increases the chance that students will remember and apply it in meaningful ways. There are many ways to modify the model to guide students to learn words in a thorough, sequential manner. The following is one way to use the technique.

Materials:

» short passage or article (display copy and 1 copy for each student)

» chart paper

» marker

» reproducible: Frayer Model graphic organizer, page 132

Process: Follow these steps:

1. Introduce a key concept or vocabulary word from a fiction passage or a nonfiction article. Ideally, articles should be based on topics students are studying during whole-class instruction, which will deepen content-area knowledge as well as knowledge of reading strategies. Over time, choose a variety of genres to expose students to a wide

range of texts. Focus on the words that students will need to know across time and genres.

2. Model and then brainstorm with students as many synonyms or examples of the key concept as possible. Here's how it could sound:

Teacher: *As we read today, I want you to circle any words that are unfamiliar. You may also circle words that you've seen before but are not sure what they mean.* (Read aloud the text as students follow along on individual copies. After the reading, discuss a word that one or more students circled.) *I noticed that Justin and Stephanie circled the word "texture."* (Read the sentence that includes the word to give students the context in which the word appeared. Guide them to come up with possible definitions and words that could substitute for the word. Write these in the "Synonyms" section of the display copy of the graphic organizer.)

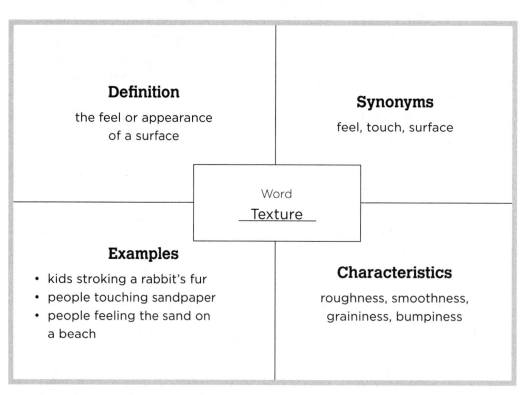

Definition
the feel or appearance
of a surface

Synonyms
feel, touch, surface

Word
Texture

Examples
• kids stroking a rabbit's fur
• people touching sandpaper
• people feeling the sand on
  a beach

Characteristics
roughness, smoothness,
graininess, bumpiness

3. List examples on the board or chart paper. Give students the opportunity to add more examples, or challenge examples that are already listed.

4. Model for and then brainstorm with students two to four characteristics or attributes of the words. The characteristics serve to deepen students' understanding of the word, along with helping create a visual image of what it looks like. Students may also make a quick sketch to depict the characteristics. Finally, provide the definition of the word so students can check their understanding. If you do not want your students to spend time figuring out what the word means using the context clues, you can define the word as the first step, so they can create synonyms and examples with greater support.

5. Now it's time to reread the passage or article. You may read it aloud as the students follow along, or students can read in pairs or independently. If you read aloud and have students follow along, you are providing a high level of support through modeling your fluency and thinking. You will also get an idea of students' readiness to read more independently by noticing their level of participation in group discussions. As students become more independent, it is a good idea to have them reread the article with a peer partner.

Use the Strategy:

- To reinforce academic vocabulary and concepts
- To guide students to think more deeply about what words mean and to make connections to other words
- To help students visualize and connect personally to words in order to derive meaning and understanding
- To enrich the reading experiences in all genres and content-area reading

Tier 2 Formative Assessments

The Frayer Model is a useful tool for gathering evidence of student learning.

✓ Jot down notes about students' level of participation and their overall attention to the task.

✓ Use the completed Frayer Model graphic organizer to gauge students' ability to express word meanings and apply their understanding by generating characteristics, examples, synonyms, and definitions.

✓ Use responses on the Frayer Model graphic organizer to assess students' ability to paraphrase and accurately define terms.

Lansdown Word Cards

When to Use: *Before and After Reading*

Purpose: *To actively involve students in the learning, teaching, and deeper understanding of key vocabulary.*

Educator Sharon Lansdown originated the set of word cards that bear her name. Each card in the set includes a context sentence from a published text to help students learn a word within an authentic reading situation. Students match a dictionary definition with the word in the context of the text, and they visualize and create an illustration to deepen their understanding of the word. Finally, students discuss the words and their usage with peers. This comprehensive word analysis strengthens understanding and word retention. Lansdown Word Cards, combined with the motivational nature of peer collaboration, bolster student achievement.

Materials:

- » student text
- » chart paper or whiteboard
- » marker
- » large index cards
- » dictionary

Process: Follow these steps:

1. Select key vocabulary words from a text students are about to read and create a display list for review prior to reading.

2. Have students fold an index card in half to prepare a Lansdown Word Card for each word. Each card should include the following:

   Inside of card

   — vocabulary word

   — part of speech in the context of the sentence

   — context sentence from the text

   — definition of the word as it is used in the sentence (Encourage students to paraphrase the definition to the best of their ability.)

   — a detailed sentence in which the word's meaning is clearly expressed

   Outside (front) of card

   — vocabulary word

   — a picture illustrating the word

> **hasty**   adjective
>
> He imagined himself carrying a pack of food and a few tools and a heavy cloth to erect a <u>hasty</u> tent.
> hasty: *quick, fast*
> I was late for school so I had to eat a hasty breakfast.

This card shows a word from Spaghetti, *by Cynthia Rylant.*

3. Have students work with you or a partner to share word cards. When pairs work together, one student acts in the role of the teacher and reviews the word and the picture. The partner tries to figure out what the meaning of the word is by looking at the illustration on the front of the card. Then students work together to review all the features of the word as displayed on the card.

The following characteristics are what make Lansdown Word Cards so effective:

— Each student is responsible for a limited number of words, yet learns many words based on the work of others.

— Students incorporate context sentences from the text and paraphrase their understanding of the words.

— Students look up their words in the dictionary and match the dictionary definitions directly to the context sentences.

— Students illustrate the meaning of each word, which is a powerful visual cue that shows the association that is guiding each student's learning.

— Peers teach one another to instruct/learn word meanings.

Use the Strategy:

- To increase vocabulary when reading texts across content areas
- To build students' background knowledge before they begin reading unfamiliar texts
- To deepen students' ability to summarize the key points of a text after reading

Tier 2 Formative Assessments

✓ Record anecdotal notes based on students' participation in discussions.

✓ Use students' word cards and responses as evidence of their thinking and progress.

VOCABULARY LESSON 6

Catch That Word

When to Use: *Before, During, and After Reading*

Purpose: *To provide experiences for students to learn vocabulary of varying levels of complexity through listening comprehension.*

In this strategy, inspired by the work of Beck, McKeown, and Kucan (2002), students listen for words they are studying in order to expand their vocabulary usage. This strategy increases students' word awareness and appreciation for word meanings (Richek 2005).

Materials:

» a content-area text or a text in a specific genre
» index cards
» chart paper or whiteboard
» marker

Process: Follow these steps:

1. Prepare a set of word cards for key vocabulary from the text you have selected to read aloud.

2. Display a list of the words on the board or chart paper and read aloud each word. Give one word card to each student.

3. Discuss the meaning of the words using the following options:

- Introduce the topic and title of the read-aloud selection and explain why you chose it. Tell students that today they will learn some new words, and then you will review the words with them. Afterward, reread the words and ask students to hold up the corresponding word cards as you read their words from the list.

- Read aloud the text and then review the words before rereading it. You may also write the sentence from the text where each word appears on a chart to guide students to apply their background knowledge and context clues to infer word meanings.

Use the Strategy:

- To build background knowledge before reading a text
- To strengthen students' listening comprehension and word knowledge during and after reading
- To expand vocabulary and enhance students' reading across subjects and genres

Tier 2 Formative Assessments

✔ Take notes based on how students participate in discussions as evidence of their thinking.

✔ Ask students to document their learning by writing in their vocabulary notebooks, for example, by summarizing the text using their newly learned vocabulary words.

Anything Goes

When to Use: *Before, During, and After Reading*

Purpose: *To build long-term retention of word meanings and usage by providing ongoing exposure to words.*

The value of this strategy is found in the repetition and review of challenging vocabulary words (Richek 2005).

Materials:

» display list of vocabulary words and/or individual set of words for each student

Process: Follow these steps:

1. Display a list of vocabulary words (current words for study or review words from past units) on the board and/or give each student a set. Word lists may range from 5–50 words.

2. Use a rapid-fire style of questioning to talk about the meaning of the words:

   What's the meaning of the word "perplexed"? How many syllables are in the word "hastily"? Which words have prefixes? How does a prefix help us figure out a word's meaning? What is the base word of "uneasy"? Spell "wonderful." Which word means the same thing as "fearful"? Act out the meaning of the word "bewildered."

   You can have individual students respond, or you can ask every student to indicate their response with a thumbs-up, written responses on whiteboards, and so on.

Use the Strategy:

- To build vocabulary for literary or content-area vocabulary words
- To use as a stand-alone lesson or as a great warm-up or transition activity
- To strengthen students' long-term memory of word meanings

Tier 2 Formative Assessments

✓ Jot down notes based on students' contributions and engagement during discussions.

✓ Have students write their responses and then use them as evidence of how well they are learning.

Word Storm

When to Use: *Before, During, and After Reading*

Purpose: *To enable students to periodically activate their knowledge of words they have learned but may not use often.*

Some words may have settled into students' long-term memory but may not come up in their speaking or writing. The Word Storm strategy aids in the retrieval, usage, and transfer of academic vocabulary (Klump 1994).

Materials:

- » reproducible: Word Storm, page 133 (1 copy for each student)
- » chart paper
- » marker
- » article about an area of study or a concept

Process: Follow these steps:

1. Write an area of study or a concept on the board, such as Math Words, Geography Words, Science Words, Adjectives, Verbs, Long /i/ words, and so on.

2. Distribute a Word Storm reproducible to each student. Give students a set time in which to write down as many words as possible related to the area of study or concept so they can retrieve words they have been exposed to, words they are familiar with, and words they know but they may or may not use regularly.

3. After time is up, review the words with students. Have them evaluate the lists of others in the group, which can foster higher-order thinking if it forces some students to justify the thinking behind their word choices.

Use the Strategy:

- ■ To expand vocabulary and enhance content-area vocabulary
- ■ To activate prior knowledge and help students to connect prior knowledge
- ■ To encourage students to make meaningful predictions about the text they are about to read

- To encourage students to evaluate their understanding of words and motivate them to seek new knowledge

Tier 2 Formative Assessments

✓ Use students' completed Word Storm reproducible to assess their understanding of vocabulary words.

✓ Observe students' ability to apply skills independently during peer interactions. Take notes that document students' independent application of skills.

Vocabulary Self-Collection

When to Use: *Before, During, and After Reading*

Purpose: *To involve students in the learning of new words.*

Students take part in choosing the words they want to learn, discuss why they chose specific words, and agree upon words for a classroom collection. This strategy guides students to make personal connections, understand the meaning of words, and apply them in everyday conversations and writing (Haggard 1986).

Materials:

» text about a current topic of study

» chart paper

» marker

Process: Follow these steps:

1. Choose a topic that students are currently learning about and then select a text that corresponds with it. Students should have some familiarity with the topic.

2. As you introduce the text, explain to students that they will take part in developing their own lists of words to learn and will come together as a group to agree upon the ten most important words for the week.

3. Preview the text with students and begin the process of selecting words they would like to learn. When you first introduce this strategy, model your thinking for choosing and adding an important word to your list. For example, the discussion of a reading about land and resources in social studies might sound like this:

Teacher: *As I looked over the text, I noticed some words in bold print. One of the words I noticed was "climate." I have heard of that word, but I am not sure what it means—so I am going to write it down. I also noticed two more terms—"renewable resource" and "non-renewable resource"—and I am wondering what they mean. I remember that the prefix non- means "no or not," so I figure these will explain the different kinds of resources that an environment has. I will add them to my word list. I also noticed the word "climate" is repeated a few times in the text, so I know that it will be an important word to know.*

4. Read the text as a group. Stop every so often to give students a chance to identify any words they would like to add to their list. Continue until the text is completed.

5. Give students time to look back at the text to help them complete their word list.

6. Group or pair students and have them share their words with one another. Each student should be prepared to defend his or her word choices.

7. After students have shared their lists, engage them in a discussion to agree upon ten words for the whole group to explore for the week.

Use the Strategy:

■ To expand students' general vocabulary skills and deepen their knowledge of content-area vocabulary

■ To activate students' background knowledge

■ To encourage students to connect personally with the vocabulary to promote deeper comprehension

Tier 2 Formative Assessments

✓ Your notes on students' participation during discussions will provide valuable information about their progress.

✓ Study students' personal word lists for valuable insight and evidence of their thinking. Their reasons for selecting the words reveal significant information about prior knowledge and understanding of words and concepts.

✓ At the end of each week, do a quick assessment of students' ability to apply their understanding of the words they selected. For example, you can have students create sentences, or you can provide sentences and ask them to fill in blanks using context and their word list as a guide.

Predict-O-Gram

When to Use: *Before and After Reading*

Purpose: *To introduce and use vocabulary to help students make predictions about a story.*

The Predict-O-Gram encourages students to use critical thinking skills, such as making predictions and self-monitoring their comprehension. It allows you to preview vocabulary and find out what students know before they begin a unit or a reading activity. It also gives students the opportunity to apply vocabulary and practice their academic speaking skills by revealing their predictions and retelling the story (Blachowicz 1986).

Materials:

» fiction selection (display copy and/or 1 copy for each student)

» reproducible: Predict-O-Gram, page 134 (1 copy for each student)

» index cards or sticky notes

Process: Follow these steps:

1. Select vocabulary from a story to activate students' thinking about making predictions and to create a word list. Choose vocabulary based on the following story elements: setting, characters, events, problem, and solution.

2. Hand out a copy of the Predict-O-Gram reproducible to each student. Ask students to make a prediction about the story based on your word list. They will categorize each word based on the corresponding story element and then sort the words accordingly.

3. Have students share their predictions through discussion and/or by writing their predictions down.

4. Read the story to students as a read-aloud or as a shared reading where you read as they follow with their individual copies. You may also select a text that students can read on their own and have them read it silently.

5. After reading, revisit the original predictions and make changes as necessary.

Tier 2 Instructional Modification

Present the words to students on index cards or sticky notes and have them sort the words before reading the text. Then ask students to make their predictions based on their placement of the words along the Predict-O-Gram organizer. After reading the story, work with students to adjust their predictions as necessary and then have them write a summary using the vocabulary and story elements from the Predict-O-Gram reproducible.

Use the Strategy:

- To introduce vocabulary
- To strengthen students' ability to use key vocabulary to make predictions and set a purpose for reading
- To encourage students to make connections between words and meaningful predictions
- To organize students' thinking in ways that guide them to use vocabulary
- To structure the steps needed for students to summarize the main ideas of a story

Tier 2 Formative Assessments

✓ Jot down notes based on what you observe about your students' participation to record concrete evidence of their thinking and progress.

✓ Use students' completed Predict-O-Gram reproducible to document their ability to make meaningful predictions.

Chapter 5

Fluency

Fluency is the ability to read words accurately and with the appropriate expression and rate as we connect to the text. As students move on to the middle grades, they are required to read and quickly comprehend increasingly complex materials. Fluency is closely linked to comprehension, so older students who lack fluency benefit from explicit instruction to build their fluency skills. In the typical middle-grade classroom, however, fluency is not usually part of the instruction. By third grade, most students have mastered learning how to read, so the focus turns to reading to learn. Yet some students still struggle to read, and they require additional time to interact with language in order to extend their vocabulary acquisition. This chapter will focus on ideas for strategic instruction that can provide supplemental support for students who need additional instruction in fluency.

One way to guide students in grades 3–5 to read fluently is to have them read a variety of texts at their independent reading level. As Richard Allington (2006) states: "We want to make sure that readers are engaged in lots of high-success reading and that we support them by modeling and demonstrating how good readers think while they read. This includes how they pay attention to words, how they think about pronunciation, and how they notice those little things writers do that tickle us."

The Five Pillars of Fluency

As we model and demonstrate what good readers do, we must keep in mind that as we read aloud to students, we are also modeling what fluent readers do. Here are five key points to keep in mind when modeling fluency:

Fluency and the Common Core State Standards

The CCSS state that fluency requires rapid, automatic decoding as well as attention to meaning and language syntax. Throughout the standards, comprehension goals address fluency through specific curriculum goals for fluent reading (e.g., recognizing and using punctuation, reading in phrases, pausing appropriately, using appropriate word stress and intonation to make reading expressive, and reading at a good rate). Fluency is an important skill that requires instructional attention across the grade levels (Fountas & Pinnell 2001).

1. Rhythm weaves through all of the components for successful fluency. It is the tempo, the beat, and the pacing of what we read. For example, a fluent reader reads a few words within one breath—as opposed to pausing after each word, which sounds robotic and perfunctory.

2. Speed in reading is not everything. In fact, I emphasize the contrary. I tell my students that in order to construct meaning, it's not the speed that's important. What counts is the rhythm, along with how much the reader understands after the reading.

3. Accuracy is key, but fluent readers also need to develop the ability to read words automatically in order for the rhythm of fluency to occur.

4. Expression refers to reading aloud in a voice that has the sound and rhythms of natural speech. Young readers often overemphasize words or read with no expression at all. It is important for readers to apply the appropriate expression. The author's use of punctuation and other text features function as cues for readers that guide their intonation and emphasis.

5. Once the preceding four pillars of fluency are in place, students can begin to apply active comprehension strategies (NICHD 2000).

When Students Struggle With Fluency

Identifying students who struggle with fluency is not difficult. Their reading is uneven and often lacks expression. It is apparent that these students focus their attention on

Reading, Fluency, and a Caution About Sustained Silent Reading

Silent reading is a key component of instruction in the middle grades, which makes sense. We strive to prepare our students to become independent, successful readers; reading silently with stamina and comprehension is a large component of achieving this goal. However, when we consider how best to incorporate silent reading into our instruction, there are a few things to consider.

Struggling readers need a lot of time to read. Yet asking these students to spend time reading silently on their own can mask the fact that they are not really reading. Struggling students often lack the strategies they need to sustain the rhythm of reading; therefore, they do not have the ability to combine the skills in order to read fluently to construct meaning (Allington 2009).

each word, or a few words at a time, rather than on constructing complete ideas as they read. They frequently ignore punctuation; they read sentences in a fragmented manner, without pausing between sentences. As a result, their comprehension suffers. In addition, students are expected to read more, and more complex, texts as they progress through grades 3–5. This increased workload makes it especially difficult for students who read slowly and awkwardly to keep up with the grade-level expectations. The laboriousness of their reading often results in a lack of motivation to read. Reading becomes too hard. Without the proper strategies to empower them, these students wonder what the use of reading is, but we teachers know that we can offer effective strategies to help.

As Allington (2009) states, "The research indicates that interventions must focus on substantial increases in the volume of high-accuracy reading that struggling readers do if fluency problems are to be overcome." Allington further explains that interventions that lead to successful reading experiences should do the following:

- Provide students with books and texts they can read easily, accurately, fluently, and with understanding.
- Include guided reading within shared reading experiences at the instructional level.

- Model explicit, powerful demonstrations of decoding, self-regulating, and comprehension strategies.

- Include repeated reading (15–20 minutes per day) that focuses on fluency and comprehension.

- Drop repeated reading after a few weeks and provide struggling readers with additional time to practice reading meaningful, easy-to-read texts (necessary to close the gap between grade-level expectations and students' personal levels of performance).

- Work to enhance the volume of reading across the school day.

Fluency and Tier 2 Instruction

Students who require supplementary Tier 2 fluency instruction typically need to have additional exposure to teacher modeling of smooth fluency patterns. In addition to hearing effective fluency patterns, they need practice in reading and hearing their own voices. Students who struggle with fluency often read without noticing punctuation, so their reading is interrupted by awkward pauses, which causes their comprehension to break down. And some students need additional practice in reading high-frequency words to help the flow of their reading patterns. Tier 2 fluency instruction is about strengthening students' ability to develop fluency so they may transform the words on the page into mental images that help them construct meaning from a text.

According to Rasinski (2000), all effective fluency instruction includes the following three primary goals:

- To help students read words accurately, rapidly, and effortlessly

- To help students read with appropriate expression and rates of fluency

- To guide students to the ultimate goal of constructing meaning from text

Typically, effective strategic instruction does not happen in the whole-class setting in grades 3 through 5. Students develop efficient fluency through their natural reading experiences and repeated exposure to read-alouds, shared reading experiences, and independent reading within real-world applications. Some students, however, need continued instruction to hone their fluency skills.

Effective strategic instruction can connect students' current level of performance with specific strategies that strengthen the fluency skills they need to succeed. Use the chart on the next page to help you match your students' needs with the fluency strategies in this chapter.

If students' performance reveals ...	Then try ...	To ...
accurate but laborious decoding	Rapid Word Recognition, pp. 92–93 Quick Read and Match, pp. 94–95	strengthen word-level fluency and the ability to read words in context with ease.
difficulty with reading words automatically	Rapid Word Recognition, pp. 92–93 Quick Read and Match, pp. 94–95	instill a stronger visual memory for important words.
mostly word-by-word reading with pauses after each word	Tracking Sentence Fluency, pp. 95–96 Repeated Reading, pp. 96–97	encourage the creation of meaning rather than just reading words in isolation.
satisfactory decoding but limited expression and ability to read in a smooth rhythm	Repeated Reading, pp. 96–97	increase students' ability to read with meaningful phrasing.
strong expression when speaking but difficulty connecting the flow of spoken language to the flow of text when reading	Repeated Reading, pp. 96–97 Choral Reading, p. 97	strengthen the ability to read with rhythm and expression.

FLUENCY LESSON 1

Rapid Word Recognition

When to Use: *Before or After Reading*

Purpose: *To increase students' background knowledge and memory of familiar words.*

The aim of this activity is to get students to easily recognize familiar words when reading, so they can focus on meaning rather than on decoding (Carreker 2005).

Materials:

- » chart paper or whiteboard
- » marker
- » a text to read to students
- » timer
- » a text to read aloud*

* *You may use this strategy without reading a text. You can simply keep a word list visible for students to use to practice fluency.*

Process: Follow these steps:

1. Prepare a rapid word list of four rows of six words each. Choose words that connect to students' background knowledge and content-area vocabulary, but which have posed difficulty for them in the past. (If you are doing this activity with a text, select words from it.) Pay close attention to the Category 2 words, identified by Beck and her colleagues (2002) as highly functional words commonly found in literary texts. The sample below involves third graders who are learning about Japan.

   Today, we are going to read a short article about how pearl divers in Japan used to dive for oysters that held precious pearls. I noticed that some of the words in this text are also words we've read in other texts. I wrote these words down on this word list. Listen and watch as I read the first row: "hundred, beneath, surface, ocean, tradition, generation." Now I'm going to point to the words again, and this time I'd like you to read them with me.

   Read through the first row of words with students. Then have them read the words without you. Continue in this manner for the rest of the rows.

2. Set a timer for 1–3 minutes to motivate students to read the words before the time is up. Students' rate of reading should increase as they become more accurate in reading the words.

3. Read the article with students.

Tier 2 Formative Assessments

✔ Take notes on how well students are able to read the article.

✔ Record students' word accuracy on a per-minute basis. Graph their progress for quick feedback.

Quick Read and Match

Purpose: *To preview and review students' accuracy and automaticity in reading key words and vocabulary.*

The idea here is to allow students to draw upon their background knowledge, which enables them to read wtih fluency and understanding.

Materials:

> » a text to read to students

> » timer

> » sheets of paper

Process: Follow these steps:

1. Create a Quick Read and Match Recording Sheet: Write a numbered list of vocabulary words from the text you've selected that you want students to read fluently. See the sample list at right from an article on Japanese pearl divers.

   Create another list on the sheet. Randomly write each numbered word and three other visually similar words (see below).

1	hundred
2	diver
3	beneath
4	deep
5	form
6	place
7	grain
8	remove
9	when
10	gem

1	hinder, honey, hunter, hundred
2	dove, hover, liver, diver
3	beneath, because, underneath, became
4	sleep, depth, steep, deep
5	from, dorm, form, forms
6	please, plays, lace, place
7	green, rain, stain, grain
8	remodel, move, remove, removal
9	then, where, when, hen
10	germ, hem, gem, gentle

2. Make a copy of the word lists for each student and distribute. Have students read each set of words and then circle the word that appears on both lists. Set the timer for 1–3 minutes to encourage students to read accurately and completely before the time is up.

3. Discuss the meaning of the words in context to bolster students' understanding of what the words mean and to expand their background knowledge.

Tier 2 Formative Assessment

✔ Record each student's percentage of words read accurately per minute on the word lists. As you gather enough data, you can graph the results to monitor students' progress.

FLUENCY LESSON 3

Tracking Sentence Fluency

Purpose: *To guide students to group words together in order to visualize what is happening in the text.*

The aim is to get students to see that words come together to form ideas and describe events.

Materials:

» sheets of paper
» reading material at students' independent reading level
» pencils in different colors

Process: Follow these steps:

1. Prepare a sheet of sentences from reading material at the students' independent reading level; leave room underneath the sentences so students may mark the text to show how they are grouping words together. Copy a sheet for each student.

2. Have students read the sentences and then use colored pencils to link the words into meaningful phrases. For example, a fluent reader would read the following sentence by grouping the words into the following phrases: "Seen from space/ Earth is almost covered by/blue oceans." A reader who pauses after almost each

word like this: "Seen from/space/Earth/is almost/covered/by/blue/oceans" is clearly not demonstrating fluency.

3. To demonstrate the various ways that fluency can be expressed, ask students to read all the marked-up sentences with you.

Tier 2 Formative Assessments

✔ Make notes of what you observe about your students' oral expression and fluency.

✔ Save students' marked-up sheets as documentation of their fluency progress.

✔ Ask students to sketch a quick image in the margin of the sheet to depict what they visualize as they read each sentence.

FLUENCY LESSON 4

Repeated Reading

Process: *To eliminate word-by-word reading with limited expression and to support reading with accuracy, rate, and prosody (expression).*

This strategy is perfect for students whose oral language and ability to decode words outpaces their ability to read sentences and paragraphs (Opitz & Rasinski 1998).

Materials:

» text at students' instructional level (print version with or without audio version)

Process: Follow these steps:

1. Select a text at the students' instructional level.

2. Have students listen to the text. This can be a teacher read-aloud or an audiobook.

3. Ask students to listen to the text a second time while reading along silently.

4. Then have them read the text aloud. Note the number of words they read correctly per minute. Afterward have students finish reading the text.

5. Check students' comprehension by having them share the basic elements of a fictional text: setting, characters, events, problem, and solution. If

the text is nonfiction, have students share the basic information of who, what, where, when, and why.

Tier 2 Formative Assessments

✔ Take notes about students' performance and progress.

✔ After a few sessions using this strategy, you can begin to create a graph to document the number of words per minute your students can read correctly.

FLUENCY LESSON 5

Choral Reading

Purpose: *To encourage students to connect the flow of spoken language with the flow of text when reading.*

Reading aloud with others helps students practice phrasing and intonation. The goal is to make sure that students are phrasing the words together as they read (Opitz & Rasinski 1998).

Materials:

» text at students' instructional level

Process: Follow these steps:

1. Select a text at students' instructional reading level.

2. As students read along on their individual copies, read sections of the text aloud, modeling appropriate rate, phrasing, intonation, and prosody.

3. Make sure that your voice can be heard over students' as you model the appropriate rate, phrasing, intonation, and prosody.

Tier 2 Formative Assessments

✔ Take notes on your students' participation, noting whether they are reading along with proper phrasing, following along visually, and able to discuss the text following the reading.

✔ You may add an additional follow-up by having students make a sketch or write a sentence to summarize the reading. This is another way to check that their phrasing has resulted in the ultimate goal of reading for meaning.

Chapter 6

Comprehension

Reading comprehension moves a reader beyond isolated skills and abilities that are needed to be a successful reader. Comprehension is a complex process that moves the focus from learning skills such as decoding, fluency, and vocabulary to a blending of these skills into the active process of gaining meaning from text. Successful comprehension allows readers to think more deeply about the information they are reading. They begin to read more naturally as they understand the text, analyze the information, apply new knowledge to what they already know, and then create new understandings that push their thinking forward. Comprehension is the ultimate goal of all reading experiences.

It's All About Comprehension

Research on comprehension is grounded in studies of what effective readers do every time they read. Reading is an active process in which readers open their minds to allow themselves to interact with the text and with the author in ways that deepen their learning, opinions, and understanding of facts. Effective readers construct, predict, question, revise, and evaluate the information as they read in order to confirm and deepen their understanding.

According to Pinnell and Fountas (2007), the following three strategic actions guide a reader's thinking:

Thinking within the text: Literal understanding achieved through maintaining fluency, monitoring understanding based on text details, and summarizing

Thinking beyond the text: Making predictions, making connections, making inferences, and synthesizing new information

Thinking about the text: Analyzing, evaluating, and critiquing the text

As we strive to propel our students to be independent thinkers, readers, and learners, we must take a long look at our instruction. We must align high-quality core instruction with intentional teaching to support students to read with a deep level of comprehension. This is not a new concept. In 1978, the eminent Russian psychologist Lev Vygotsky offered a strong research-based theory that made a crucial distinction between a student's individual performance capability and what he or she was capable of doing with support. Vygotsky described two levels of development:

Level 1: This is the student's present level of performance. It describes what the student is capable of doing without any help from others. This is the student's independent level, his or her comfort zone.

Level 2: This is the students' potential level of performance. It describes what the student is potentially capable of doing with help from other people or teachers.

Vygotsky posited that a gap exists between these two levels of performance; he called it the zone of proximal development (ZPD). He believed that when students were given support from other, more knowledgeable people, they could then apply knowledge and skills that they already possessed. However, the knowledge must be appropriate for their levels of comprehension. Students cannot learn anything that is too complicated without support to strengthen their abilities. When students do attain their potential, they can continue learning more complex, higher level material. Vygotsky believed, ". . . children grow into the intellectual life of those around them" (1978).

The idea of supporting students to think at higher levels also appears in the work of Benjamin Bloom and his colleagues (Bloom, Engelhart, Furst, Hill, & Krathwohl 1956). They outlined a hierarchy of thinking levels that teachers have been using for decades to organize curriculum and guide students toward independent thinking at higher and deeper levels. Anderson and Krathwohl (2001) have since revised Bloom's Taxonomy in a powerful way to support 21st-century learning.

When Students Struggle With Comprehension

Students have trouble making sense of what they read for a variety of reasons, and these reasons are not always easy to decipher. Those students who do struggle need to be guided toward a greater awareness of their own thinking. They need to learn how to organize their thoughts and how to express them successfully—things that proficient readers take for granted.

Sometimes students struggle simply because they do not gain enough from whole-class instruction for their current level of performance to improve. If helping students achieve is a matter of fine-tuning the instructional process, then Tier 2 instruction can help put them on the right track.

Although all the comprehension strategies in this chapter may be used to nurture the skills needed to be a deeper thinker and successful reader, here are a few suggestions to guide your instructional planning.

Comprehension and Tier 2 Instruction

It is easy to spot students who are struggling with comprehension. Typically, they avoid reading whenever possible. And when they must read, they are clearly disconnected from the text and less than enthused. These students say that it is difficult to remember or follow what is going on in the text. They are either your readers who take a very long time to read because they are trying so hard—or who finish reading in record time because they are not really reading the text. When engaging in a discussion about the text, these students are not able to share key parts, characters, or facts, or to formulate their own opinions about the information they read. In addition,

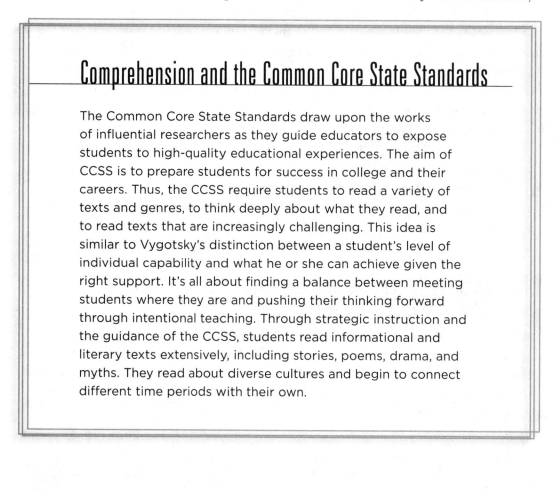

Comprehension and the Common Core State Standards

The Common Core State Standards draw upon the works of influential researchers as they guide educators to expose students to high-quality educational experiences. The aim of CCSS is to prepare students for success in college and their careers. Thus, the CCSS require students to read a variety of texts and genres, to think deeply about what they read, and to read texts that are increasingly challenging. This idea is similar to Vygotsky's distinction between a student's level of individual capability and what he or she can achieve given the right support. It's all about finding a balance between meeting students where they are and pushing their thinking forward through intentional teaching. Through strategic instruction and the guidance of the CCSS, students read informational and literary texts extensively, including stories, poems, drama, and myths. They read about diverse cultures and begin to connect different time periods with their own.

these students are not able to create visual images to help them comprehend.

The pacing of the whole-class setting may not allow students struggling with comprehension the additional practice they need. And more often, students need additional small-group instruction to review and develop the active reading strategies needed for successful comprehension. Tier 2 instruction provides these students with the explicit instruction and additional practice to help them apply these necessary comprehension skills.

Effective strategic instruction can connect students' current level of performance with specific strategies that strengthen the comprehension skills they need to succeed. Use the chart below to help you match your students' needs with the comprehension strategies in this chapter.

If students' performance reveals . . .	Then try . . .	To . . .
difficulty determining importance when reading	Leveled Questioning, pp. 102–104 Chunk, Stop, Think, pp. 104–106 Possible Sentences, pp. 123–125	increase their focus on sections of the text
difficulty comprehending text at a basic, literal level	Question-Answer Relationship, pp. 113–116 Question-Answer-Detail, pp. 122–123	deepen their level of thinking and understanding
difficulty summarizing	Chunk, Stop, Think, pp. 104–106 Sketch to Stretch, pp. 118–121	visualize and identify key ideas
lack of background knowledge	Experience Text Relationship, pp. 106–109 Possible Sentences, pp. 123–125	build upon background knowledge, make new connections
limited higher-level thinking	Leveled Questioning, pp. 102–104 Question-Answer Relationship, pp. 113–116	foster deeper thinking
lack of metacognition and limited use of active reading strategies	Reciprocal Teaching, pp. 110–112 Insert, pp. 117–118 Directed Reading/Thinking Activity pp. 125–126	encourage self-monitoring and regulation of learning and understanding

Leveled Questioning

When to Use: *Before and After Reading*

Purpose: *To encourage students to increase their critical thinking through asking and responding to literal, interpretive, and evaluative questions.*

This revised model of Bloom's Taxonomy reflects the needs of today's outcome-oriented learning environments; therefore, students are encouraged to become active thinkers within the learning process. For example, the category of "Remember" replaces "Knowledge" to indicate that students must do something in order to remember the knowledge presented to them (Anderson & Krathwohl 2001).

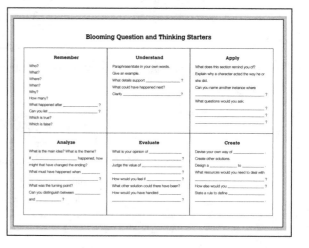

Materials:

» passage at students' independent reading level (display copy and 1 copy for each student)

» sheet of paper or poster board

» pen or marker

» reproducible: Blooming Question and Thinking Starters, page 135 (display copy and/or 1 copy for each student)

» reproducible: Thinking Categories Organizer, page 136 (1 copy for each student)

» reproducible: Anecdotal Notes, page 129 (1 copy for you)

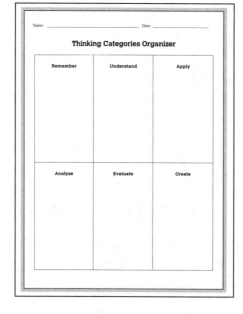

Process: Follow these steps:

1. To introduce this strategy, select reading material that is at students' independent reading level; this allows you to focus strictly on strategic thinking and comprehension. Once students are accustomed to leveled questioning, this strategy will work beautifully as you challenge them with instructional texts to help them reach grade-level expectations.

2. Use the Blooming Question and Thinking Starters reproducible to prepare between 10–15 leveled questions on a sheet of paper. If you want the whole group to complete the questions, enlarge a copy of the reproducible to display.

3. Engage students in a shared reading of the passage or have them read it independently.

4. Following the reading, have students sort the leveled questions using the Thinking Categories Organizer.

5. Remind students that this strategy is not about answering the questions. Tell them that, in fact, you do not want them to answer the questions at all! You only want them to think about the types of questions they are.

6. Together with students, read through the questions and then have them sort the types of questions, explaining how they chose a category for each question.

7. Once all the questions have been sorted and discussed, students can then begin to answer them, taking notice of the type of thinking they will need to use to respond. For example, questions in Level 1, the "Remember" category, are those in which the answer is found right there in the text. As you move along the categories of questions, your students must use more of their background knowledge, judgment, and opinions.

Use the Strategy:

- To introduce or review a topic
- To activate students' awareness that there are various levels of thinking
- To direct students to ask questions that deepen their level of understanding
- To provide experiences that allow students to think about a topic from various perspectives
- To get students to think critically, while justifying their thinking

Tier 2 Formative Assessments

✔ Use the Anecdotal Notes reproducible to keep to keep track of each student's specific comments and participation during class discussions.

✔ Create an exit pass for students to complete before the lesson is over.

Have them answer one to three comprehension questions about the text. For example, here are a few leveled questions for a text about the 13 colonies:

- *Where did the people who settled in the 13 colonies come from?*

- *What can you conclude about the colonists from the information on pages 10–13?*

- *If you were a settler of one of the 13 colonies, which colony would you prefer to live in? Why?*

- *What are the reasons that the colonists came to North America?*

- *What was life like in the 13 colonies?*

- *Suppose you could spend a day going to school in the colonies— how would you feel and why?*

- *How would you compare the Native Americans and the English colonists?*

- *What facts show that the Native Americans welcomed the settlers at first?*

- *What judgment can you make about the reasons the colonists wanted to be free?*

- *Do you agree with the colonists who did not want to pay taxes?*

✔ Ask students to generate a question of their own regarding the text or topic. You can have them code the question by identifying the level of thinking their question requires in order for someone to answer it.

COMPREHENSION LESSON 2

Chunk, Stop, Think

When to Use: *Before, During, and After Reading*

Purpose: *To guide students to pace, monitor, and deepen their comprehension of a text.*

Students need to stop to think about a text: They need to become aware of what they believe the author is communicating, and what they think will happen next. Students also need to stop to ask questions, make predictions, and make connections in order to feel actively engaged in the process of reading (Duke and Pearson 2002).

Materials:

» passages at students' instructional and independent reading levels (display copy of instructional passage and 1 copy of independent passage for each student)

» sticky notes

» chart paper

» marker

Process: Follow these steps:

1. Select a reading passage (or give students a choice among texts you have pre-approved). Mark several stopping points in the text with sticky notes (paragraph breaks are easy places to stop). If you are having students read silently, make sure the text is at their independent reading level. If you are using this as a shared reading activity, use an instructional-level text.

2. Model reading the text and then stopping. Draw a line in the text to indicate the stopping point. Notice that in the sample for "Spaghetti" in *Every Living Thing* by Cynthia Rylant on the next page, the student chunked her reading after each paragraph and began to jot down her thoughts about each section.

   The student and I completed the first section together. After reading, we circled some key words and phrases, such as *evening, quietly, crumbling bricks, rotting wood,* and *wished for some company.* The student derived that the character was lonely, and she wrote that in the margin.

3. Think out loud in two-to-five-word phrases to paraphrase what the section of text is mostly about. Jot your thinking on chart paper or the board. Then continue reading to the next stopping point.

4. At the end of the reading, use your notes to guide you to paraphrase and summarize the most important parts of the reading.

5. On another day, guide students as they interact with the text and supply most of the thinking.

6. Once you feel students are ready, allow them to read a passage independently and apply the strategy.

Use the Strategy:

- To guide students to monitor their comprehension by processing one section of a text at a time

- To help students break down the reading task into manageable sections in order to monitor themselves effectively and make meaning of a text

- To help students connect to and think more deeply about the information in a text

Tier 2 Formative Assessments

✓ Use students' copies of the text after they have indicated stopping points and shown their thinking as they read through it.

✓ Take anecdotal notes based on students' performance.

✔ Create a double-notes sheet in which you provide specific text evidence and then have students infer the theme/main ideas. This sheet will be a good assessment of the students' ability to infer meaning and themes along with providing opportunities for them to analyze text evidence. The samples below are based on a lesson using "Spaghetti" by Cynthia Rylant:

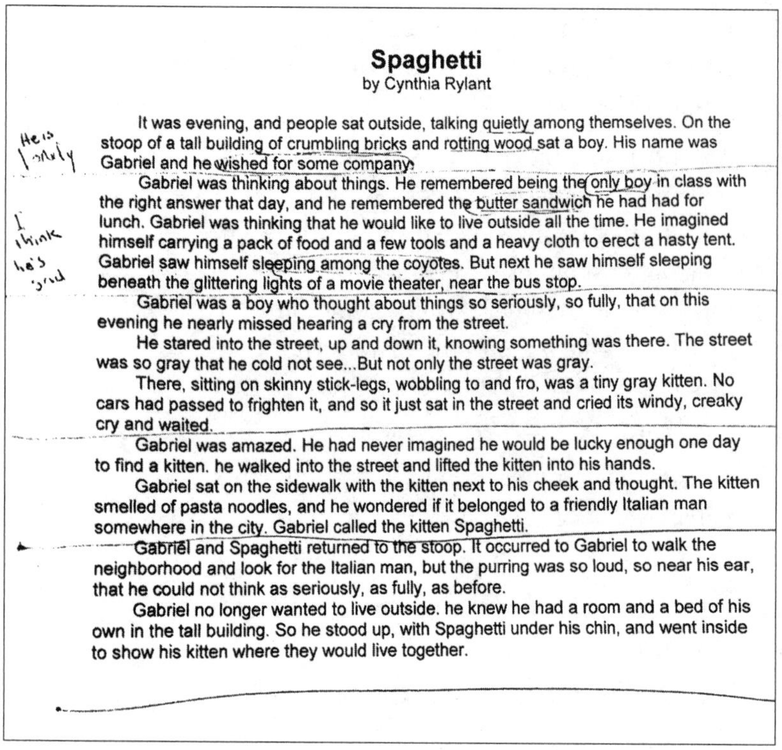

Spaghetti
by Cynthia Rylant

[handwritten: He is lonely]

It was evening, and people sat outside, talking quietly among themselves. On the stoop of a tall building of crumbling bricks and rotting wood sat a boy. His name was Gabriel and he wished for some company.

[handwritten: I think he's sad]

Gabriel was thinking about things. He remembered being the only boy in class with the right answer that day, and he remembered the butter sandwich he had had for lunch. Gabriel was thinking that he would like to live outside all the time. He imagined himself carrying a pack of food and a few tools and a heavy cloth to erect a hasty tent. Gabriel saw himself sleeping among the coyotes. But next he saw himself sleeping beneath the glittering lights of a movie theater, near the bus stop.

Gabriel was a boy who thought about things so seriously, so fully, that on this evening he nearly missed hearing a cry from the street.

He stared into the street, up and down it, knowing something was there. The street was so gray that he cold not see...But not only the street was gray.

There, sitting on skinny stick-legs, wobbling to and fro, was a tiny gray kitten. No cars had passed to frighten it, and so it just sat in the street and cried its windy, creaky cry and waited.

Gabriel was amazed. He had never imagined he would be lucky enough one day to find a kitten. he walked into the street and lifted the kitten into his hands.

Gabriel sat on the sidewalk with the kitten next to his cheek and thought. The kitten smelled of pasta noodles, and he wondered if it belonged to a friendly Italian man somewhere in the city. Gabriel called the kitten Spaghetti.

Gabriel and Spaghetti returned to the stoop. It occurred to Gabriel to walk the neighborhood and look for the Italian man, but the purring was so loud, so near his ear, that he could not think as seriously, as fully, as before.

Gabriel no longer wanted to live outside. he knew he had a room and a bed of his own in the tall building. So he stood up, with Spaghetti under his chin, and went inside to show his kitten where they would live together.

Student sample

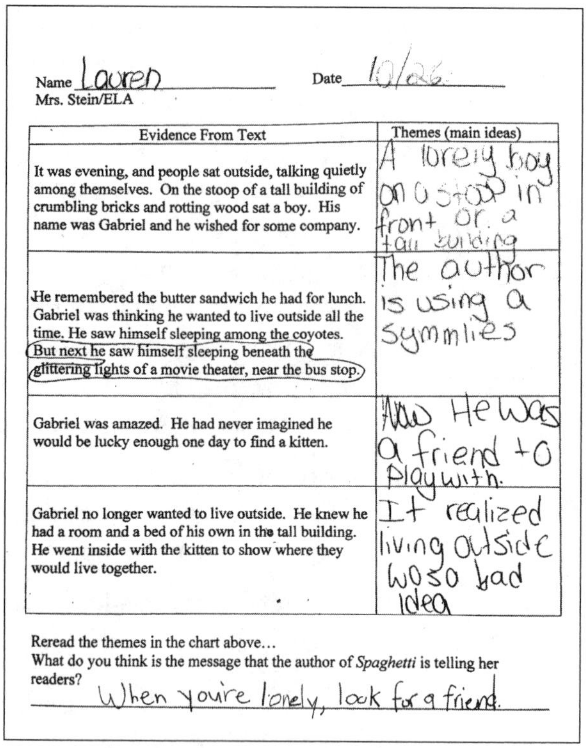

Name **Lauren**   Date **10/26**
Mrs. Stein/ELA

Evidence From Text	Themes (main ideas)
It was evening, and people sat outside, talking quietly among themselves. On the stoop of a tall building of crumbling bricks and rotting wood sat a boy. His name was Gabriel and he wished for some company.	*A lonely boy on a stoop in front of a tall building*
He remembered the butter sandwich he had for lunch. Gabriel was thinking he wanted to live outside all the time. He saw himself sleeping among the coyotes. But next he saw himself sleeping beneath the glittering lights of a movie theater, near the bus stop.	*The author is using a symmiles*
Gabriel was amazed. He had never imagined he would be lucky enough one day to find a kitten.	*Now He was a friend to play with.*
Gabriel no longer wanted to live outside. He knew he had a room and a bed of his own in the tall building. He went inside with the kitten to show where they would live together.	*It realized living outside waso bad idea*

Reread the themes in the chart above...
What do you think is the message that the author of *Spaghetti* is telling her readers? *When you're lonely, look for a friend.*

Double-notes sheet

COMPREHENSION LESSON 3

Experience Text Relationship

When to Use: *Before, During, and After Reading*

Purpose: *To guide readers to connect their background knowledge with main ideas in a text.*

Students learn to connect what they know to a text and determine importance as they read (Au, 1979).

Materials:

» high-quality fiction; content-area books, articles, and other nonfiction texts

» sticky notes

» sheets of paper

Process: Follow these steps:

1. Select a text that will allow your students to make predictions and connections. When introducing this strategy, it is best to use high-quality fiction texts. As students become accustomed to the process, content-area books, articles, and other nonfiction texts are also very powerful to incorporate. Mark stopping points with sticky notes. These stopping points should allow you to smoothly model your thinking as you connect the text to your background knowledge and deepen comprehension. Create a series of comprehension questions for each section of the text. Duplicate a set for each student.

2. Preview the text by discussing the title and any text features. Ask students to make a prediction based on the title and any text features such as illustrations, summaries, graphics, and so on. The purpose of this first prediction is not only to set a purpose for reading, but also to have students confirm or refine this original prediction throughout the reading.

3. Engage students in a shared, choral, or independent reading of the text until they reach the first predetermined spot. This activity should be completed as a shared reading until you see that students are ready to determine stopping points independently. Scaffold the process over time by modeling, then choosing the stopping points together, and finally having students choose their own.

4. Before reading the text, distribute a copy of the comprehension questions and encourage students to make connections, generate questions, revise or confirm predictions, and make inferences based on text details (see the sample lesson based on *Just a Dream*, by Chris Van Allsburg on the next page).

5. At each stopping point, pose the leveled questions and ask students to support their thinking with evidence from the text. Be sure to insert students' questions that arise in the moment.

6. Reading resumes to the next stopping point. The thinking cycle continues until each section has been discussed and the text is completed.

Use the Strategy:

■ To set a purpose for reading by having students preview the text and make predictions based on text features

■ To break down the reading process by creating stopping points to allow for reflection

■ To guide students toward deeper thinking through making predictions, making connections, asking questions, and monitoring their comprehension

Tier 2 Formative Assessments

✓ Keep notes describing students' participation during group discussion.

✓ Use students' responses to the comprehension questions to record their understanding of the text and application of strategies.

Sample Experience Text Relationship Lesson

Text: *Just a Dream* by Chris Van Allsburg

Genre: Fiction

This book is especially well suited to the spring and Earth Day, but it can be read at any time during the year to exercise students' critical reading skills. All students can relate their personal experiences to taking care of the environment.

Possible Themes:

- Environmental awareness: reduce, reuse, recycle
- Character change
- Significance of dreams

This sample lesson uses the theme of environmental awareness as the main idea. See the Stopping Point Organizer I created for *Just a Dream* on page 109.

Stopping Point #1:

- Guide students to think about the author's purpose and perspective.
- Provide an opportunity for students to find text evidence to support their response to the Synthesize and Infer question.
- Encourage students to evaluate some of Walter's character traits at the beginning of the text.

Stopping Point #2:

- Encourage readers to make predictions and justify their thinking by providing text evidence.

Stopping Point #3:

- Continue to guide students to evaluate Walter's character traits.
- Guide readers to evaluate how Walter has changed and to synthesize information to answer the question.
- Motivate students to connect the text to their own personal experiences.

Stopping Point Organizer

Title: _Just a Dream_   Author: _Chris Van Allsburg_

Stopping Point #1

Synthesize and Infer: What message do you think the author is hoping readers understand when reading about Walter's dream? _____

_____

What clues from the text help you make this inference? _____

_____

Write two character traits that describe Walter at the beginning of the story.

Character Trait #1	Character Trait #2

Stopping Point #2

Make a Prediction: How will Walter's dream affect his attitude about taking care of the environment?

_____

_____

What evidence from the text, or your own schema, helped you make this prediction?

_____

Stopping Point #3

What are two character traits that describe Walter at the end of the story?

Character Trait #1	Character Trait #2

Explain how Walter's character changed from the beginning of the story to the end of the story. Use details from the text to support your answer. _____

_____

_____

What does this story remind you of? _____

_____

Reciprocal Teaching

When to Use: *Before, During, and After Reading*

Purpose: *To guide students' basic comprehension through making predictions, summarizing, asking questions, and clarifying.*

Created by Palinscar and Brown (1984), reciprocal teaching is a comprehension strategy that guides readers in making predictions, summarizing, asking questions, and clarifying. It provides opportunities for students to think more deeply about what they read by applying active thinking processes. In addition, reciprocal teaching supports students' social development by enabling them to apply these active reading strategies within the context of cooperative and social learning.

Materials:

» text at students' instructional level that lends itself to making predictions and clarifying

» index cards and markers

Process: Follow these steps:

1. Begin by reviewing the four types of thinking strategies you want students to use as they read the text. Model your thinking as much as possible when you first introduce this strategy, as demonstrated in the sample below.

   Careful readers use many different strategies when they are reading. You can use the strategies in any order when you read.

   *When we **predict**, we ask ourselves, "What will this section be about? Why do I think that?"*

   *When we read, we **clarify** by asking ourselves if there are any words or phrases that are confusing. We can also ask ourselves if there are phrases or sections of the reading that are confusing. If we are confused, then we go back and reread parts of the text to help us understand.*

   *As we are reading, we stop to think about what we are wondering about. Sometimes, even when we understand the text, we stop to think about our reading—not because we have any questions or predictions, but just to summarize what we've read so far, to make sure we're clear about what we've read. When we can choose the important ideas and put them in our own words—in other words, when we **summarize**—that shows we understand what we are reading.*

*Another thing careful readers do is to **visualize** as they are reading. They picture what's going on, or they connect to something they've seen or read about before. Visualizing helps us concentrate and think more deeply about what we are reading.*

Gradually release responsibility to students, allowing them to "be the teacher" and model their thinking to the group.

2. You can make Reciprocal Teaching Discussion Cards by writing the names of the four strategies on index cards. Place the cards faceup in the center of the table, allowing any student to chime in at each strategy discussion time. For example, when you hold up the Predict card, allow any and all students to add their input about predictions. Placing all cards on the table, faceup, is effective once students understand what each thinking strategy is about. This allows them to practice the flexibility that proficient readers exhibit all the time—the ability to utilize any of these strategies at any time to deepen their understanding. If students are not yet savvy about each strategy, then introduce one strategy at a time. For example, if you just want to work on predictions, display only that card and weave the strategy into your conversation. See the sample cards for the Predict, Clarify, Summarize, Visualize, and Question strategies below.

Predict

What do you think this section will be about? Why?

What evidence from the text supports your prediction?

Clarify

Are there any words or phrases that you find confusing?

Are there sections of the reading that you do not understand?

Reread the parts of the text that will help you understand it.

Summarize

Please summarize the reading in your own words.

What have you read so far?

What important events have happened so far?

Visualize

What image do the words create in your mind?

What are you picturing in your mind?

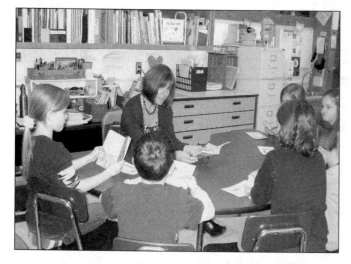

My colleague, Jeanne Hall, works with small groups for targeted comprehension skills during her readers' workshop instructional block. In this photo, she is using the Reciprocal Teaching strategy with a group.

Add the other strategies as students become more comfortable. As you continue to read the text, follow the same procedure for each of the strategies. For example, you can ask, "Who can summarize?" "Who has a question?" "Who came across a confusing word or idea?"

Another way to implement the Reciprocal Teaching approach is to give each student a card that states which strategy he or she will focus on during the reading. For example, the "Predictor" will share predictions, the "Summarizer" will summarize, and so on. Each student can still have the opportunity to apply his or her thinking by eliciting ideas from peers. For example, the "Predictor" might ask peers if they would like to add anything to his or her ideas. This allows each student to practice one strategy, but he or she will be exposed to, and begin to think about how to use, the other strategies as well.

Use the Strategy:

- To introduce or review content-area topics

- To help students determine importance when summarizing literary or informational texts

- To guide students to monitor their own thinking before, during, and after reading

Tier 2 Formative Assessments

✔ Document students' performance through anecdotal notes. Jot down quotes to show evidence of students' thinking, along with observations about their general participation.

✔ Ask students to write a quick summary about what they have read on a sheet of paper or in a reading notebook.

✔ Create an exit pass that asks students to describe how one of the strategies helped them on that particular day. For example, if making predictions was the strategy focus, you can write, "How did making predictions help you understand what you read today?" As students become more independent, you can ask, "How does the Reciprocal Teaching strategy help you be a stronger reader?"

Question-Answer Relationship

When to Use: *Before, During, and After Reading*

Purpose: *To help students develop self-questioning skills and deeper comprehension.*

Students learn to consider information from the text as well as their own background knowledge when reading. This strategy is ideal for deepening comprehension because it guides students to know where to seek answers to questions. Sometimes the questions can be answered directly in the text; other times readers need to apply their prior knowledge to varying degrees (Raphael 1984).

This strategy explicitly shows students that comprehension involves combining their background knowledge with text details. It does so by categorizing specific types of questions and guiding readers to know where to seek answers.

Question-Answer Relationships (QAR)

Category	Type of Question
In the Book	**Right There:** The answer can be found in one place in the text.
	Think and Search: The answer can be found by combining information from several different places in the text.
In My Head	**Author and Me:** The answer can be found by connecting the reader's background knowledge with evidence from the text.
	On My Own: The answer cannot be found in the text. The reader must find it based on his or her previous experiences.

Materials:

»   passage with five to ten comprehension questions

»   Question-Answer Relationships Chart, pages 115–116

»   reproducible: Blooming Question and Thinking Starters, page 135

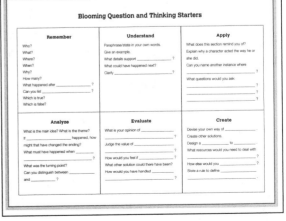

Process: Follow these steps:

1. You may introduce the categories of question types in the order you prefer. For example, you may first introduce In the Book questions and then In My Head questions on two separate days; or for older students, you may decide to introduce all four types of questions in one day.

2. Select a short passage. Choose the text based on the instructional level of your students. Make sure to vary the genre between informational and literary. You may choose a passage with questions that follow it, or you can easily generate five to ten questions using the Blooming Question and Thinking Starters as a guide.

3. Read the text aloud and model thinking about the background knowledge that is triggered by your reading. Here's how a fourth-grade discussion about a passage on Sacagawea might go:

   Teacher: (reading text) *"Sacagawea sat in the boat with her baby. She was on a long journey home. Sacagawea thought about her home. It was the beautiful land of the Shoshone people. When Sacagawea was a child, there had been a war. She had been taken far from her home. Now Sacagawea was going west with two explorers, Lewis and Clark"* (Riley 2000). (Stop here to think aloud and to guide students to make connections to activate background knowledge.) *Yes, I remember we read about how Sacagawea was kidnapped as a young girl and taken from her homeland in the West. Years later, she saw Lewis and Clark, who were going on an expedition to explore the west. But there was a problem.*

   Arturo: *Lewis and Clark didn't know how to communicate with the natives in the West, so Sacagawea went with them to translate.*

   Teacher: *Right, and she helped them survive on their journey. So let's read a little bit about what happened on that expedition.*

4. Then read the comprehension questions and engage students in the thinking needed to respond. Use verbal thinking hints, along with a visual aid, such as the QAR Chart, to help students apply the strategy.

   Teacher: *Here is the first question: "Why did Lewis and Clark name a river after Sacagawea?" I don't remember reading about why they named the river after her, but we can infer the reason. The text tells us that Sacagawea helped them find food, saved their food when they were in the water, and watched over them. She did so many helpful things for them,* *and I know they were thankful. I also know that when people are thankful, they like to do something nice back. So, do you think that could be why they named a river after Sacagawea?* (Through further discussion, you would guide the group to code this question Author and Me, because it required them to use some clues from the text and some ideas from their own background knowledge.)

Question-Answer Relationships Chart

	Question Type	What I think . . .	What I can do . . .
In the Book	*Right There* What kind of food did Sacagawea find for Lewis and Clark?	I remember seeing this information on page 6 of my reading.	Scan, reread, and notice key words from the question in the text. Ask if the answer I find in the text makes sense.
	Think and Search When Sacagawea reached Shoshone country with Lewis and Clark, how did the native people react?	I remember reading about that. On one page, I saw an illustration that showed Sacagawea dancing. And in the next two paragraphs there were details to show how the Shoshone chief welcomed her. I need to combine information from all these different places in the text.	Reread and skim, find key words and ideas, paraphrase, summarize and synthesize.

continued on next page

continued . . .

In My Head	Author and Me	In the text, I remember reading that she saved the food and supplies in the wild waters. I already know that wild waters can be dangerous. I also know that "brave" describes someone who does something even if she is afraid. I can connect what I know with the clues from the text. What I know fits perfectly with this text.	Make predictions, inferences, and connections; reread, think about what I know and how it connects to what the author is saying.
	What is a character trait that can describe Sacagawea?		
	On My Own	I don't remember seeing anything directly in the text. I need to research this from another text and make my own connections to answer it.	Scan the text for key words from the question; make predictions, inferences, connections; think about what I know.
	How did Sacagawea meet Lewis and Clark?		

Use the Strategy:

- To encourage students to ask and respond to questions that deepen their comprehension

- To prepare for contents-area tests by reviewing material

- To deepen students' level of comprehension through questioning and responding

Tier 2 Assessments

✔ Review anecdotal notes.

✔ Create an exit ticket to check that students understand what each question type means and how it can help them when reading and answering questions.

Sample exit ticket:

1. Answers to Right There questions are found right there in _____ (*title of text*).

2. Answers to Author and Me questions are found by using your _____ (*own experience*) and information in the _____ (*text*) to make inferences.

Insert

When to Use: *During Reading*

Purpose: *To guide students to monitor their own comprehension by coding the text.*
This will help students develop an internal dialogue as they read that will allow them to realize when comprehension breaks down (Duke and Pearson 2002).

Materials:

» Insert Codes poster (display copy: chart paper or poster board and marker; student copy: sheet of paper, marker)

» copies of a text for marking (1 for each student)

» sticky notes

Process: Follow these steps:

1. Choose a text based on a topic students are studying or a topic of interest to spark students' motivation to read.

2. Create a class poster showing the insert codes and also make individual copies for students. Sample codes are shown below.

Insert Codes	
X	I thought differently.
+	New information
!	WOW, this was interesting.
?	I don't understand.
*	Very important
zzz	This was not interesting. I already knew that.

Allow students to create their own symbols as they become comfortable with this strategy.

3. Distribute a copy of the text you have chosen and the insert codes to students. Then think aloud as you read the text and mark it with the codes as shown below:

Teacher: *As I read the part that said the* Titanic *hit the iceberg, I coded that with a checkmark because I already knew that. But when I got to the part that said there weren't enough life jackets or lifeboats, I coded that with a star because I think that is an important reason why so many people died.*

4. Give students the opportunity to mark up copies of a text whenever possible; otherwise they may use sticky notes or make notes in their notebook.

Use the Strategy:

■ To help students value their thinking as they read

■ To help students determine important information in text

■ To guide students to develop the thinking they need to connect with a text

■ To strengthen students' memory of interesting and important facts in the text

Tier 2 Assessments

✔ Document students' participation through anecdotal notes.

✔ Collect students' coded text and responses as evidence of their thinking.

✔ Have students convert their codes into complete sentences.

✔ Create an exit pass by asking students, "How does using codes when you're reading help you remember what you read?"

COMPREHENSION LESSON 7

Sketch to Stretch

When to Use: *During and After Reading*

Purpose: *To visually demonstrate comprehension.*

This strategy gives students the opportunity to clarify their understanding of important events and information in a text, and then to summarize their understanding through illustrations and words. Sketching helps students organize their thinking as they build metaphors, symbolic thinking, and analogies, and synthesize key points from the text (McLaughlin and Allen 2002).

Materials:

» a literary or nonfiction text that complements a topic of study

» sheet of paper

Process: Follow these steps:

1. Have students read a text or listen as you read it. Before reading, ask students to fold a sheet of paper into four quadrants and number each quadrant from 1–4 to encourage sequential thinking. Tell them to sketch key information sequentially as it appears in the text.

2. If you are reading the text aloud, stop periodically to let students sketch key parts. Note that some students may wait until you complete the passage to start sketching.

3. At the end of the reading, allow time for students to complete and fine-tune their sketches. They may add key words or captions to the pictures as an additional means of expressing their ideas visually and in writing. Their words can also guide them when they will use their sketches to complete a written summary on the back of their sheet.

4. Then have students summarize the key points of the text by using their sketches as a springboard for organizing their thinking. Students may summarize orally or in writing—your choice. On the next two pages, see student samples based on *Tornado* by Betsy Byars.

Use the Strategy:

- To encourage students to deepen their comprehension through visualization
- To guide students to summarize a text in a sequential and logical way
- To provide opportunities for students to evaluate and identify key points in a text

Tier 2 Formative Assessments

✔ Collect students' sketches with or without captions to see how well they are able to determine importance in a text.

✔ Gather students' written summaries based on their sketches as evidence of their ability to summarize key information in a sequential manner.

Front of student #1 Sketch to Stretch

Bot 1 <u>Tornado</u> A Tornado struck Tornado Alley. Pete's roof gets torn of of his house. To pete, it ~~was~~ happened in a blink.	**Box 2** Pete, his mother and father^{and} walked out back into their backyard. A tree with a tire swing was on the ground lying down. A mysterious doghouse was next to the well.
Box 3 A Black Dog in the doghouse was shivering. Pete wanted to know if he could own that Dog.	**Box 4** Even Although that Black dog wasn't his, he temperarily named him Tornado. Tornado shakes Pete's father's hand.

Back of student #1 sketch sheet shows the written summary of his sketch after listening to the story.

Front of student #2 Sketch to Stretch

Tornado

A dad, a boy, and a mom were in their kitchen, eating breakfast, when a tornado happend. The kitchen roof fell off. The dad, the mom, and the son went outside to see what had happend. Almost everything was broken. There was a doghouse that has never been there before. The doghouse made a noise. There was a dog in the doghouse. The boy gave food and water to the dog.

Back of student #2 reflects her written summary

Question-Answer-Detail

When to Use: *Before, During, and After Reading*

Purpose: *To apply self-questioning as a means of motivating students to set a purpose for reading and achieve deeper levels of comprehension.*

In the beginning, you set the purpose of the reading and then direct students' questioning to meet that goal. This strategy is perfect for guiding students' higher-level thinking skills as they construct meaning from text (Duke and Pearson 2002).

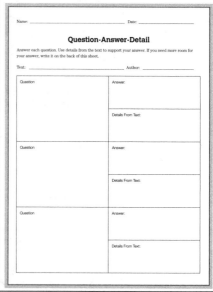

Materials:

»   a nonfiction text or literary text

»   reproducible: Question-Answer-Detail, page 137 (1 copy for each student)

Process: Follow these steps:

1. When you introduce the strategy, provide the questions for the first column of the chart on the Question-Answer-Detail reproducible and continue to do so until students become familiar with it. After handing out the reproducible, explain to students that they will find the answers to the questions in the first column and write them in the second column. In the same column, they should supply details to support each answer. This will guide students to read for deeper understanding.

    At right is a sample created to go along with the book *Grandfather's Journey* by Allen Say.

2. Preview the text with students to prepare them to make predictions and get their minds ready to learn more about the topic.

3. Then go over the questions with students. Explain that referring to the questions as they read will help them comprehend key ideas in the text. You may even wish to have students take notes consisting of

key words. After reading, they can use their notes to fill in the Answer box.

4. After the reading, allow time for students to fully answer the questions. If you have time, review their responses.

You can also adapt Question-Answer-Detail by having students generate their own questions after previewing the text. They can use the Blooming Question and Thinking Starters reproducible on page 135 to encourage them to think at higher levels.

Use the Strategy:

- To encourage students to go back into a text to find evidence for their thinking
- To review key information from a text for a test
- To increase students' attention to text details

Tier 2 Formative Assessments

✓ Collect students' completed Question-Answer-Detail graphic organizers.

✓ Take notes based on students' responses and participation.

✓ Create a quick comprehension quiz based on reading (see Quick Checks, page 55).

COMPREHENSION LESSON 9

Possible Sentences

When to Use: *Before and After Reading*

Purpose: *To improve students' comprehension of content-area reading by using vocabulary to make predictions about the content.*

Students will learn to confirm, modify, and alter their original predictions (Moore & Moore 1986).

Materials:

» passage from a textbook or another nonfiction text

» reproducible: Possible Sentences Organizer, page 138

Process: Follow these steps:

1. Choose five to ten words from the selected text that are key to understanding its content but that may be unfamiliar to students. List them on the board.

2. Choose another four to six words from the text that are more familiar to students and add those words to the list as well.

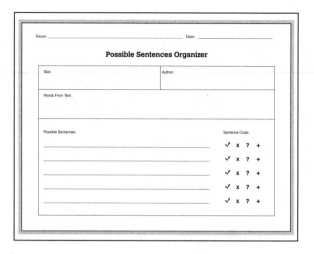

3. Read the words with the students to model accurate pronunciation and review their definitions. Be sure to include students in the discussion of the definitions—this will activate their background knowledge and help you easily assess what they already know.

4. Once you are sure students are able to discuss what the words mean, give them time to either work independently or in pairs to develop three to five sentences that predict what the text is about. Tell students to use at least two words from the list in each sentence. Write a few sentences on the board.

5. Direct students to read the text independently or as a group. After reading the text, have students revisit their sentences and revise them to align exactly with the content of the text. Add students' new or revised sentences to the list. (This new information will not necessarily include any of the five to ten words on your original list.)

6. Encourage students to return to the text and have them check their statements for accuracy. They should code each of their sentences accordingly; for example:

> ✔ Confirmed and accurate
>
> X Inaccurate
>
> ? Not sure
>
> + New information learned

Use the Strategy:

- To review a specific topic in preparation for a test
- To introduce a topic of study and activate students' background knowledge

- To deepen students' comprehension of any nonfiction text or topic

Tier 2 Formative Assessments

✓ Document students' participation and understanding through anecdotal notes.

✓ Collect students' completed Possible Sentences Organizers.

✓ Create a quick comprehension quiz based on the reading.

COMPREHENSION LESSON 10

Directed Reading/Thinking Activity

When to Use: *Before, During, and After Reading*

Purpose: *To encourage students to make predictions using text evidence (clues from the author), make meaningful connections, and confirm or change their predictions.*

This activity can increase students' awareness of how their thinking changes as they continue to read (Duke and Pearson 2002).

Materials:

» a literary text

» reproducible: Directed Reading/Thinking Activity Organizer, page 139 (1 copy for each student)

Process: Follow these steps:

1. Select an independent-reading-level text if students are reading silently. Choose a text at students' instructional level if you are reading it together. Designate stopping points in the text.

2. Preview the text by focusing on the title, cover, and any text features that will give clues to what the text is about. Have students discuss their predictions and the reasons behind them.

3. Distribute a copy of the reproducible to each student before you begin to read

and tell students to jot down their predictions.

4. Read to the first stopping point in the text as a shared reading. Ask students to review their predictions, make new predictions, and explain the reasons behind their thinking. Have them jot down their thoughts on the reproducible.

5. Continue reading together to the next stopping point and review students' thinking again. Continue in this manner until the end of the text. As students become more familiar with the strategy, allow them to read silently.

6. Ask students to reflect on their predictions with partners or the group. Focus their attention on what they were thinking before, during, and after reading the text. Discuss how their thinking changed and why it changed. Make sure to have students include specific details from the text to support their thinking.

Use the Strategy:

■ To encourage students to monitor their own comprehension every time they read

■ To make students more independent when applying active reading strategies

Tier 2 Formative Assessments

✔ Take notes based on students' participation in group discussions.

✔ Collect students' completed Directed Reading/Thinking Activity Organizer as evidence of their thinking.

Reflective Teacher's General Checklist

	Yes	No
Before Teaching Action: Did I plan lessons around the necessary themes, topics, standards, objectives, and essential understanding?		
During Teaching Action: Did I monitor the learning expressions and behaviors of my students and make on-the-spot modifications to lessons?		
After Teaching Action: Did I evaluate and learn from my students' actions and performance?		
Future Teaching Action: Will I use what I learn from my students' actions and performance to guide the planning of future lessons and units of study?		

Lesson Reflection Checklist

	Yes	If not, why?
Were students active all the time?		
Were students attentive all the time?		
Did students seem to be learning?		
Did students enjoy the lesson?		
Were students motivated?		
Were students engaged in the learning activities and phases of the lesson plan?		
Did the lesson go according to your plan?		

Anecdotal Notes

Student	Objective	Performance	Next Steps

Name: _____

Date: _____

List-Group-Label

Words:

Label: _____

These words form a group because _____
_____
_____

Label: _____

These words form a group because _____
_____
_____

Label: _____

These words form a group because _____
_____
_____

Label: _____

These words form a group because _____
_____
_____

Name: _____ Date: _____

Synonym Links

Write the vocabulary word on the line. Fill in the links with synonyms for the vocabulary word.

Word: _____

Word: _____

Word: _____

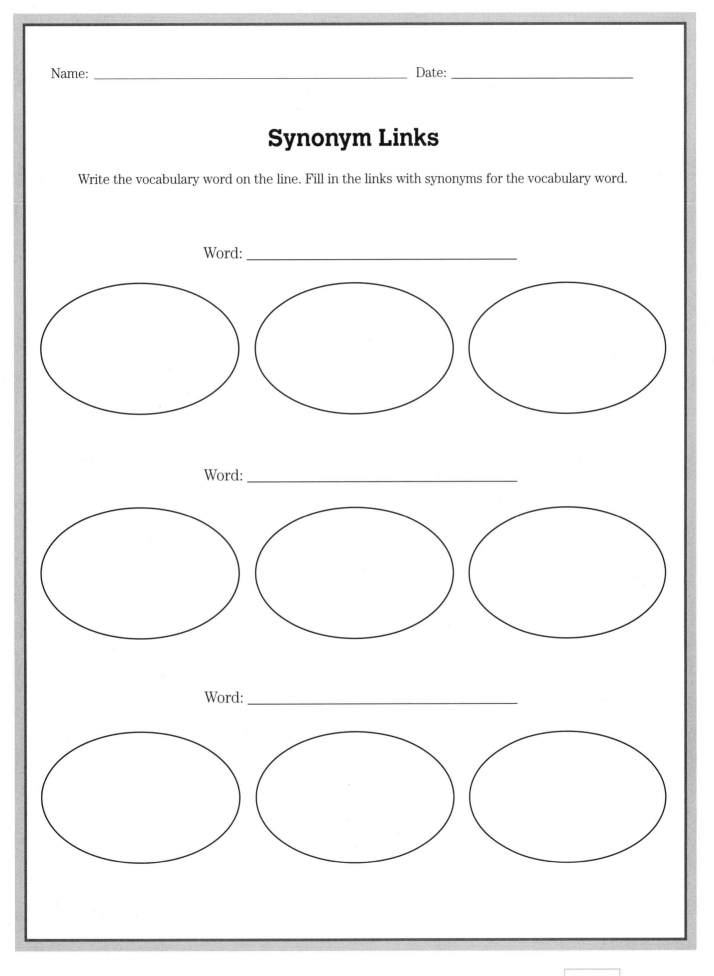

Name: _____ Date: _____

Frayer Model

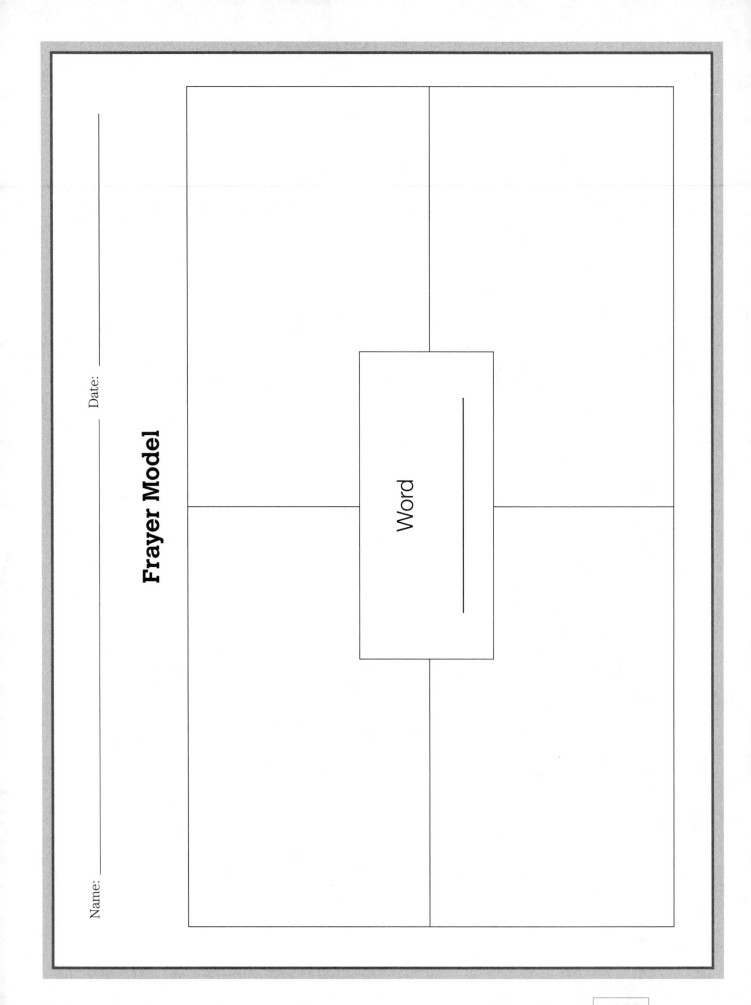

Word
_____

Name: _____

Date: _____

Word Storm

Word	Personal Connection	Prediction	Actual Meaning of Word

Name: _____ Date: _____

Predict-O-Gram

Text:	Author:			
Vocabulary From the Text:				
Setting:	Characters:			
Events:				
Problem:	Solution:			

Blooming Question and Thinking Starters

Remember

Who?

What?

Where?

When?

Why?

How many?

What happened after _____ ?

Can you list _____ ?

Which is true?

Which is false?

Understand

Paraphrase/state in your own words.

Give an example.

What details support _____ ?

What could have happened next?

Clarify _____ ?

Apply

What does this section remind you of?

Explain why a character acted the way he or she did.

Can you name another instance where _____ ?

What questions would you ask:

_____ ?

_____ ?

_____ ?

Analyze

What is the main idea? What is the theme?

If _____ happened, how _____ might that have changed the ending?

What must have happened when _____ ?

What was the turning point?

Can you distinguish between _____ and _____ ?

Evaluate

What is your opinion of _____ ?

Judge the value of _____ ?

How would you feel if _____ ?

What other solution could there have been?

How would you have handled _____ ?

Create

Devise your own way of _____ .

Create other solutions.

Design a _____ to _____ .

What resources would you need to deal with _____ ?

How else would you _____ ?

State a rule to define _____ .

Name: _____ Date: _____

Thinking Categories Organizer

Remember	Understand	Apply
Analyze	**Evaluate**	**Create**

Name: _____ Date: _____

Question-Answer-Detail

Answer each question. Use details from the text to support your answer. If you need more room for your answer, write it on the back of this sheet.

Text: _____ Author: _____

Question	Answer:
	Details From Text:
Question	Answer:
	Details From Text:
Question	Answer:
	Details From Text:

Name: _____

Date: _____

Possible Sentences Organizer

Text:	Author:

Words From Text:	

Possible Sentences:

Sentence Code:

✓	✗	?	+
✓	✗	?	+
✓	✗	?	+
✓	✗	?	+
✓	✗	?	+

_____

_____

_____

_____

_____

Name: _____

Date: _____

Directed Reading/Thinking Activity Organizer

Text: _____

Author: _____

Stop and Jot #1

I predict _____

I think this because _____

Stop and Jot #2

I will review my prediction. Was my prediction accurate, or do I need to change it?

Now my prediction is _____

because _____

Stop and Jot #3

After reading, I realize _____

My thinking changed about the beginning of the text to the end of it because _____

References

Allington, R. L. (2006). *What really matters for struggling readers: Designing research-based programs* (2nd ed.). Boston: Allyn & Bacon.

Allington, R. L. (2009). *What really matters in fluency: Research-based practices across the curriculum.* Boston: Allyn & Bacon.

Anderson, L. W., & Krathwohl, D. R. (Eds.). (2001). *A taxonomy for learning, teaching, and assessing: A revision of Bloom's Taxonomy of educational objectives: Complete edition.* New York: Longman.

Au, K. H. (1979). Using the experience-text-relationship method with minority children. *Reading Teacher* (32), 677–679.

Beck, I. L., McKeown, M. G., & Kucan, L. (2002). *Bringing words to life: Robust vocabulary instruction.* New York: Guilford Press.

Bender, W. N. (2009). *Beyond the RTI pyramid: Implementation issues for the first five years.* Bloomington, IN: Solution Tree Press.

Blachowicz, C. L. (1986). Making connections: Alternatives to the vocabulary notebook. *Journal of Reading, 29*, 643–649.

Blachowicz, C., & Fisher, P. (2002). *Teaching vocabulary in all classrooms* (2nd ed.). New Jersey: Pearson Education, Inc.

Bloom, B. S. (Ed.), Engelhart, M. D., Furst, E. J., Hill, W. H., & Krathwohl, D. R. (1956). *Taxonomy of educational objectives: Handbook I: Cognitive domain.* New York: David McKay.

Byars, B. (1996). *Tornado*. New York: HarperCollins.

Carreker, S. (2005). Teaching reading: Accurate decoding and fluency. In J. R. Birsh (Ed.), *Multisensory teaching of basic language skills* (2nd ed.). Baltimore, MD: Paul H. Brookes Publishing Co.

Common Core State Standards (2010). The National Governors Association and the Council of Chief State School Officers.

Cowie, B., & Bell, B. (1999). A model of formative assessment in science education. *Assessment in Education, 6*, 101–116.

Darling-Hammond, L., & Bransford, J. (2005). *Preparing teachers for a changing world: What teachers should learn and be able to do.* San Francisco: Jossey-Bass.

Davis, L. B., Fuchs, L. S., Fuchs, D., & Whinnery, K. (1995). Will CBM help me learn? Students' perception of the benefits of curriculum-based measurement. *Education and Treatment of Children, 18*(1), 19–32.

Deno, S. L., & Mirkin, P. K. (1977). *Data-based program modification: A manual.* Reston VA: Council for Exceptional Children.

Dewey, J. (1933). *How we think.* New York: D. C. Heath.

Donovan, S., & Bransford, J. D. (2005). *How students learn: History, mathematics, and science in the classroom.* Washington, DC: National Academies Press.

Duke, N. K., & Pearson, D. (2002). Effective Practices for Developing Reading Comprehension. In A. E. Farstrup & S. J. Samuels (Eds.), *What research has to say about reading instruction* (3rd ed., 205–242). Newark, DE: International Reading Association.

Fountas, I. C., & Pinnell, G. S. (2001). *Guiding readers and writers grades 3–6: Teaching comprehension, genre, and content literacy.* Portsmouth, NH: Heinemann.

Frayer, D. A., Frederick, W. C., & Klausmier, H. G. (1969). A schema for testing concept mastery. Technical Report 16, University of Wisconsin.

Fuchs, L. S., & Fuchs, D. (2007). A model for implementing responsiveness-to-intervention. *Teaching Exceptional Children, 39*(5), 14–20.

Fuchs, D., Mock, D., Morgan, P. L., & Young, C. L. (2003). Responsiveness-to-intervention: Definitions, evidence, and implications for the learning disabilities construct. *Learning Disabilities Research & Practice, 18*, 157–171.

Good, R. H., Simmons, D. C., & Kame'enui, E. J. (2001). The importance and decision-making utility of a continuum of fluency based indicators of foundational reading skills for third-grade high-stakes outcomes. *Scientific Studies of Reading, 5*, 257–288.

Goodman, K. (1969). Analysis of oral reading miscues: Applied psycholinguistics. *Reading Research Quarterly, 5*, 9–30.

Goodman Y., & Marek, A. (1996). *Retrospective miscue analysis in the classroom.* Katonah, NY: Richard C. Owen Publishers.

Haggard, M. R. (1986). The vocabulary self-collection strategy: Using student interest and world knowledge to enhance vocabulary growth. *Journal of Reading, 29*(7), 634–642.

Harvey, S. & Goudvis, A. (2007). *Strategies that work: Teaching comprehension for understanding and engagemen*t (2nd ed.). Portland, ME: Stenhouse Publishers.

Harvey, S. & Daniels, H. (2009). *Comprehension and collaboration.* Portsmouth, NH: Heinemann.

Herman, J. L., & Winters, L. (1994). Portfolio research: A slim collection. *Educational Leadership, 52*(2), 48–55.

Klump, M. R. (1994). Connecting vocabulary to the student's database. *The Reading Teacher, 48*(3).

Lansdown, S. (1991). Increasing vocabulary knowledge using direct instruction, cooperative grouping, and reading in junior high school. *Illinois Reading Council Journal, 19*, 15–21.

McLaughlin, M. & Allen, M. (2002). *Guided comprehension: A teaching model for Grades 3–8.* Newark, DE: International Reading Association.

Marzano, R. J. (2004). *Building background knowledge for academic achievement.* Alexandria, VA: Association for Supervision and Curriculum Development.

Marzano, R. J. (2003). *What works in schools: Translating research into action.* Alexandria, VA: Association for Supervision and Curriculum Development.

Marzano, R. J., & Carlton, L. (2010). Vocabulary games for the classroom. Bloomington, IN: Marzano Research Laboratory.

Marzano, R. J., & Pickering, D. J. (2005). *Building academic vocabulary: Teacher's manual.* Alexandria, VA: ASCD, 2005, 14-30.

Mazer, D. (2002). *The amazing days of Abby Hayes: Out of sight, out of mind.* New York: Scholastic.

Mellard, D. F., Fuchs, D., & McKnight, M.A. (2006). *Responsiveness to intervention (RTI): How to do it.* Lawrence, KS: National Research Center on Learning Disabilities.

Moore, D. W., & Moore, S. A. (1986). Possible sentences. *Reading in the content areas: Improving classroom instruction.* Dubuque, IA: Kendall/Hunt.

National Institute of Child Health and Human Development. (NICHD) (2000). Report of the National Reading Panel. *Teaching children to read: An evidence-based assessment of the scientific research literature on reading and its implications for reading instruction.* NIH Publication No. 00-4769. Washington, DC.: U.S. Government Printing Office.

National Institute of Child Health and Human Development. (NICHD) (2007). Report of the National Reading Panel. *Teaching children to read: An evidence-based assessment of the scientific research literature on reading and its implications for reading instruction.* Government Printing Office: Washington, DC.

Opitz, M. F., & Rasinski, T. V. (1998). *Good-bye round robin: Twenty-five effective oral reading strategies.* Portsmouth, NH: Heinemann.

Palinscar, A. S., & Brown, A. L. (1984). Reciprocal teaching of comprehension-fostering and comprehension-monitoring activities. *Cognition and Instruction, 2,* 117–175.

Pence, K. L., & Justice, L. M. (2008). *Language development: From theory to practice.* Upper Saddle River, NJ: Prentice-Hall.

Pinnell, G. S., & Fountas, I. C. (2007). *The continuum of literacy learning, grades 3–8: A guide to teaching.* Portsmouth, NH: Heinemann.

Raphael, T. E. (1984). Teaching learners about sources of information for answering comprehension questions. *Journal of Reading, 27,* 303–311.

Rasinski, T. V. (2000). Speed does matter in reading. *The Reading Teacher, 54,* 146–151.

Richek, M. A. (2005). Words are wonderful: Interactive, time-efficient strategies to teach meaning vocabulary. *The Reading Teacher, 58,* 414–415.

Riley, K. (2006). *Sacagawea.* New York: Houghton Mifflin.

Rylant, C. (1985). *Every living thing.* New York: Aladdin.

Say, A. (1993). *Grandfather's journey.* New York: Houghton Mifflin.

Schon, D. A. (1983). *The reflective practitioner: How professionals think in action.* London: Temple Smith.

Schumaker, J. B., Denton, P., & Deshler, D. D. (1984). The paraphrasing strategy. In Ellis, E. S., & Lenz, B. K. (1987). A component analysis of effective learning strategies for LD students. *Learning Disabilities Focus, 2,* 94–107.

Sweet, D. (1993). *Education research: Consumer guide to student portfolio* (8th ed.). Washington, DC: Office of Research and Improvement, U.S. Department of Education.

Taba, H. (1967). *Teachers' handbook for elementary social studies.* Reading, MA: Addison Wesley Publishing Co., Inc.

Tomlinson, C. A. (1999). *The differentiated classroom: Responding to the needs of all learners.* Alexandria, VA: ASCD.

Tomlinson, C. A. (2001). *How to differentiate instruction in mixed-ability classrooms.* Alexandria, VA: ASCD.

Tomlinson, C. A. & Edison, C. C. (2003). *Differentiation in practice: A resource guide for differentiating instruction, grades 5–9.* Alexandria, VA: ASCD.

Valencia, S. (1990). A portfolio approach to classroom assessment: The whys, whats, and hows. *The Reading Teacher, 43*(4), 338–40.

Van Allsburg, C. (1990). *Just a dream.* New York: Houghton Mifflin.

Vygotsky, L. S. (1978). *Mind and society.* Cambridge, MA: Harvard University Press.

Zipf, G. K. (1935). *The psycho-biology of language.* Boston: Houghton Mifflin.